DIVINE HEALING:

GIVING
God AN
OPPORTUNITY

DIVINE HEALING:

GIVING *God* AN OPPORTUNITY

DR. DOYLE JONES
with Mel Surface

TATE PUBLISHING & *Enterprises*

Divine Healing: Giving God an Opportunity
Copyright © 2011 by Doyle Jones. All rights reserved.

No part of this publication may be reproduced, stored in a retrieval system or transmitted in any way by any means, electronic, mechanical, photocopy, recording or otherwise without the prior permission of the author except as provided by USA copyright law.

Scripture quotations marked (AMP) are taken from the *Amplified Bible*, Copyright © 1954, 1958, 1962, 1964, 1965, 1987 by The Lockman Foundation. Used by permission.

Scripture quotations marked (KJV) are taken from the *Holy Bible, King James Version*, Cambridge, 1769. Used by permission. All rights reserved.

Scripture quotations marked (NCV) are taken from the *New Century Version®*. Copyright © 2005 by Thomas Nelson, Inc. Used by permission. All rights reserved.

Scripture quotations marked (NIV) are taken from the *Holy Bible, New International Version®*, NIV®. Copyright © 1973, 1978, 1984 by Biblica, Inc.™ Used by permission of Zondervan. All rights reserved worldwide. www.zondervan.com

Scripture quotations marked (NKJV) are taken from the *New King James Version®*. Copyright © 1982 by Thomas Nelson, Inc. Used by permission. All rights reserved.

Scripture quotations marked (NLT) are taken from the *Holy Bible, New Living Translation*, copyright © 1996. Used by permission of Tyndale House Publishers, Inc., Wheaton, Illinois 60189. All rights reserved.

Scripture quotations marked (NRSV) are from *New Revised Standard Version Bible*, copyright © 1989 National Council of the Churches of Christ in the United States of America. Used by permission. All rights reserved.

Scripture quotations marked (Weymouth) are from the *Weymouth New Testament*, Richard Francis Weymouth, 1912. Public domain in the United States.

The opinions expressed by the author are not necessarily those of Tate Publishing, LLC.

Published by Tate Publishing & Enterprises, LLC
127 E. Trade Center Terrace | Mustang, Oklahoma 73064 USA
1.888.361.9473 | www.tatepublishing.com

Tate Publishing is committed to excellence in the publishing industry. The company reflects the philosophy established by the founders, based on Psalm 68:11,
"The Lord gave the word and great was the company of those who published it."

Book design copyright © 2011 by Tate Publishing, LLC. All rights reserved.
Cover design by Sharee Faircloth
Cover photo by Thinkstock
Interior design by Lynly D. Grider

Published in the United States of America

ISBN: 978-1-61346-008-5
1. Religion: Christian Life: Inspirational   2. Religion: Christian Life: General
11.06.17

DEDICATION

With great delight I dedicate this book to a very special lady in my life, my wife, Cherie. Cherie has had her faith severely tried with nineteen different operations, but she continues to testify about the goodness of God. The ultimate test was cancer. Three times doctors suspected that she had cancer when they found growths in various parts of her body. The first time doctors said she had a tumor as big as a softball. We prayed and believed God. When she went back for x-rays, the tumor was gone. On another occasion, she had tumors that, when removed, proved to be non-cancerous. However, on the third occasion, she had cancer in the third stage and went through chemo, an operation, and radiation. Her oncologist, a Christian lady, did not give her a good prognosis. But after the operation and now, many years later, the doctor continues to tell her that she is a miracle.

Through it all, Cherie, has maintained her faith and her poise. She is truly amazing. I am grateful to God that He spared her. And I am certainly grateful we have seen so many miracles of healing in our ministry together and that we can continue serving God together.

TABLE OF CONTENTS

Foreword

You have chosen well in deciding to read this practical primer on divine healing as one of God's gifts for suffering men and women. In these pages, Dr. Jones offers several practical guidelines based in scriptural truths that will lead you to help your family and friends to experience all the Lord makes available to them.

One of the author's most beneficial and needed contributions in this book is that he inspires faith in the reader's spirit. This is not merely positive thinking; rather, this is biblical faith that Jones has practiced successfully in his own life year after year through hardship and difficulty. He has also inspired and observed this biblical faith in the experiences of countless thousands of people in multiplied dozens of countries around the world.

A review of Jesus's ministry while on earth reveals that He spent a good deal of His time healing people. This same practice characterized the ministry of the apostles and early church leaders after Jesus had ascended back to heaven and sent the Holy Spirit to empower believers. Jesus told his followers before His departure that they were to wait until they received the empowerment of the Holy Spirit. The power of the Holy Spirit in their lives would equip them to be useful to God in ministry.

One aspect of this multifaceted anointing of the Spirit was that they would see the sick healed in their ministry. Jesus made it quite clear that just as He had healed the sick; His followers would continue that ministry and see people healed by the power of Jesus's name. When the Holy Spirit came to empower 120 faithful believers on the day of Pentecost, the apostle Peter announced, while under the anointing of that same Holy Spirit, that this same empowerment was a promise of God to all succeeding generations of believers. Divine healing is still the promise of God for today.

Teachings on the subject of healing in both testaments make it clear that divine healing is a provision of God throughout all ages. An inclusive term used in the Bible for this work of God's grace in our lives is "gifts of healings." The double plurality of this expression emphasizes that God's intervention in our health needs can come in an endless variety of ways and the supply is limitless. Yet all too frequently, people fail to take advantage of these gifts as fully as God intended.

Some fail to enjoy all the supernatural healing that the Lord makes available to them, simply because they do not ask. Yet others ask without seriously expecting to be healed. Others think they do not deserve these blessings, or they do not want to trouble the Lord by asking. These conditions, and several others, are capably addressed in the book.

Missionary evangelist Doyle Jones presents in these pages a comprehensive mosaic of biblical teachings on this subject. His commentaries on the biblical passages are clear and concise. He skillfully explains a wide assortment of biblical teachings by relating real life experiences of people he has met during his years of ministry who were miraculously delivered from a widely diverse range of debilitating health issues. His book then is not designed as a theological treatise on the subject of healing; rather, it is intended as a practical manual to guide the reader to a correct understanding of biblical teachings.

The author demonstrates specifically how these teachings apply to health needs. He walks the reader through a series of practices, questions and doubts that frequently hinder many from receiving the full benefits of God's grace.

It has been my distinct privilege and joy to have known Dr. Jones as a close, personal friend throughout his adult life. Never has he been anything other than a man of honorable integrity, with a steadfast resolve to faithfully live out the will of God in his life. Without the slightest hesitation, I can say that I hold him in the highest of respect as a man of God. He has been wonderfully used by the Lord as an evangelist, pastor, missionary, college professor and administrator, international convention and conference speaker, author, singer and musician.

Open your mind and your heart to all that the Lord wishes to accomplish in you as you read this book. Then let Him use you as you put your renewed faith into practice by praying the prayer of faith for the healing of your family members and friends. With God all things are possible.

Dr. Larry McNeill
President, Latin America Theological Seminary/
Facultad de Teologia

PREFACE

This is the book that I have desired to write for some time. In fact, I have been writing it for a few years. At one time this book had nearly four hundred pages. You can readily tell that the book has been greatly reduced.

I am greatly indebted to my close friend Mel Surface for perusing the original manuscript and then quietly asking, "Who is your audience? Theologians or people who need healing?" At first I defended the approach I had taken, pointing out that laymen also needed to read books with more in-depth information from a theological standpoint. However, I had to call Mel a few days later with the declaration, "You just ruined a good book!" The truth is, all along as I wrote about healing, I kept having some reservations about the approach I was taking. Ultimately, I felt that Mel was right. I needed to simplify the book, reorganize it, and present the truth of a balanced approach to healing in a way that would help those who needed physical healing, as well as others who needed a better understanding of a great biblical truth.

Mel has been a help in more than one way. With his expertise as a journalist and professional writer, it made sense to ask him to edit the book. He did a great job. As a result, I think you will find this book very easy to read but, at the same time, phrased in such a way to keep the reader involved.

The essence of the message of this book remains the same. God does heal. He longs for His children to give Him the opportunity to do the impossible. He also wants us to trust Him when things do not happen according to our expectations.

Though Cherie and I have seen countless miracles in countries around the world, we have never lost the thrill of what God can do. We sometimes know and feel that God is about to do something incredible in the lives of people; however, because God is Sovereign, what He does, when He does it, and how He does it contributes to our continuing awe of His incredible wisdom and power. It is our desire that many will share in this continuing faith and wonder of a mighty God who does the impossible and that scores of individuals will experience his power personally.

Expecting the Unexpected

Barling, Arkansas, population 4,400, hugs State Highway 22 just eight miles southeast of Fort Smith. Special Sunday services were in progress at First Assembly of God, and I announced to the morning congregation that I would preach on healing that night. Nothing in the situation suggested God was going to do something incredible, but we determined to give him an opportunity. We discovered He had everything in place for a miracle.

This was April 2001, and Paula Ginn had been suffering two years from rapidly progressing multiple sclerosis. She left the morning service leaning heavily on a four-pronged cane and helped by her husband and two of their four children.

Paula was diagnosed in early 2000 after experiencing kidney and bladder problems. Surgery revealed nerve damage but did not solve her condition. Over the next few months, the disease triggered paralysis in her hand and legs, and twisting bones caused her to drag her feet. She used the cane but felt she soon would need a wheelchair.

Paula's voice was affected, and her speech became slow and slurred. Her vision began to blur, and excruciating sensitivity to light demanded she wear sunglasses—even indoors.

Though tests did not reveal why the disease advanced so rapidly, she said her doctor told her she had two years, at most, to live. Coming home with that prognosis, she collapsed on the sofa in near hysterics. She called on God as she thought of her family and friends. She prayed to die, but God had a better plan.

She testifies that He made her to know she should go back to Barling First Assembly, which she had not attended for many years. Though angry that God did not heal her at that moment, she was convinced He had told her healing would come some evening at church.

She found a welcome at the church when she and her family began attending in February, 2001. Her faith began to grow and she kept on expecting healing though her physical condition grew worse. By this time, her husband and children had to help her up and down the stairs.

She trusted God and began talking about her expectation. Some joined her in prayer and faith while others were skeptical. She says, "In my heart, I knew I would not be this way long,"

When I announced I would preach on healing, she was eager to get back to church that night. At church time, her head and legs were throbbing with pain, and her husband suggested they go the hospital emergency room. She insisted on going to church "if I have to crawl on my hands and knees to get there." Though late, they made it.

Her pain grew worse during the meeting until she agreed with her husband that she should head for the ER.

Just then, I gave the invitation to prayer for healing and, instead of leaving, she came forward. Even though she was expecting God to heal her sometime, she says she did not know what would happen that night.

She sat down for prayer because she hurt too badly to stand. When we prayed for God to heal Paula, I had no special revelation or sensation that something spectacular was going to happen. I had no word of knowledge or surge of great faith. We simply obeyed God's Word by praying for her and giving Him an opportunity to do the impossible.

Even after I laid hands on her and prayed, from my perspective, nothing like a miracle took place. Again, we gave God an opportunity by asking Paula to do something she had not been able to do.

At first, she could move only one finger. Then she began moving all of them. She raised both arms—all of this for the first time in nearly two years!

When I told her to take off her glasses, her whisper of a voice exploded into a shout, "I can see! I can see!" Next, I asked if she thought she could stand. She thought she could and she did. I asked if she thought she could walk. She said, "Yes!" and she did. Her only pain now came from the no longer needed braces. Her friend helped her to remove them once and for all.

At home that night, she walked up and down the stairs. Even before she got home, she began calling everyone she knew to tell them what God had done. Now, she says, "I can shower, run, read, cook, and be with my family."

Paula kept her appointment with a specialist a few weeks later, accompanied by her husband, daughters, and

Pastor Darryl Billingsly with his wife, Shirley. She says the doctors said, "There is a lot about multiple sclerosis we do not understand," not admitting that they had witnessed a miracle.

Perhaps the most important part of this story is how God is using what He did for Paula and her family to bring others to Christ. At least twenty-five individuals, including ten members of a Buddhist family, have come to faith in Jesus as Savior and Lord.

That is what miracles do. They glorify God and testify of Jesus Christ. They confirm His death, resurrection, and unchanging power for every generation. Miracles validate His claims. He is the Son of God. He died for sinners and rose from the dead. All power—power to forgive, to heal, to do whatever—belongs to Him. This is good news everyone needs to hear.

Paula said, "God told me that one night He would heal me if I would go to that church." Some congregations never hear preaching or teaching on healing. They seldom, if ever, experience prayer for the sick. The church that Jesus launched in the book of Acts stands in contrast to many churches today.

In Acts, they prayed that Christ would heal the sick. The book even records a specific prayer of the early church. It came during a time of persecution. Church leaders had been arrested and warned not to preach about Jesus. Instead of keeping silent, the church prayed:

"They raised their voice to God with one accord and said … 'Now, Lord, look on their threats, and grant to your servants that with all boldness they may speak Your word,

*by stretching out Your hand to heal; and that signs and won-
ders may be done through the name of Your holy Servant Jesus*
(emphasis added)'" Acts 4:29–30 (NKJV).

Paula Ginn's story demonstrates Bible precepts and the
context in which miracles can take place. God could have
healed her at home or anywhere else and at any time, but
He put her into an atmosphere conducive to expecting the
impossible. Her story can help us begin to trust God and to
give Him opportunities for miracles.

MAN'S EXTREMITY IS GOD'S OPPORTUNITY

M an's extremity is God's opportunity!"

As a young Christian, I heard Pastor Allen Sanders declare it so often and with such conviction that it burned indelibly into my spirit. It became a pillar in my Christian walk and in the evangelistic ministry God would give me.

Pastor Sanders conditioned me to look up when everything else is down. He persuaded me that when human help and hope slam into the wall of impossibility, God can take over. He convinced me I should believe and encourage others to believe God, to expect Him to act when all else is exhausted. He made me want to step out in faith, lean on God, and do what otherwise we never could.

When I started preaching, I searched the Scriptures in vain for the pastor's favorite maxim. The quote actually is attributed to John Hamilton, Lord Belhaven, in a 1706 speech to the Scottish Parliament. Still, it presents a biblical principle. God seems to delight in opportunities to do the impossible.

It was no accident that Jesus taught one Sabbath in a synagogue where he saw a severely stricken woman. Her twisted frame had kept her doubled over for eighteen years, but on that otherwise unremarkable day, her impossibility met the Master of possibilities. Her extreme, hopeless condition actually was the opportunity of a lifetime. Jesus healed her! Her condition dissolved in His compassion. Everything was wrong, but it was right for a miracle.[1]

Bartimaeus, the blind man mentioned in Mark's gospel (chapter 10:46–52), would not have been healed if his extreme condition had not sparked a desperate plea. Jesus was passing his way, the last time he would walk the Jericho road before His crucifixion. Bartimaeus kept on calling out, despite efforts to keep him quiet. Jesus heard him and healed him. Man's extremity became God's opportunity.

Through more than forty years of ministry, I have witnessed thousands of people healed in every kind of circumstance. Planting churches outside the United States, we have prayed for the sick every night in campaigns that continued for months. In this country also, we have seen incredible miracles of healing of every dimension. People have been healed as we joined in prayer by telephone or outdoors on a busy street. I have seen people get out of hospital beds and go home after prayer though their doctors had given them no hope of recovery.

I began to preach healing with a very limited understanding. The Bible presents Jesus as the Healer, so that is what I preached. I read various books that dealt with healing and preached what I learned from others who had great healing miracles in their ministry.

Most of the books I studied put heavy responsibility on the individual in need. It seemed that, if a person prayed long enough and hard enough and quoted enough scripture, God was obligated to heal. The emphasis on what the individual does sometimes bordered on humanism. It set the stage for awful guilt if the miracle did not unfold as prescribed.

The opposite extreme taught that healing is strictly in the sovereignty of God. He could heal if He wanted to but seldom does. This left little place for faith and prayer. I could see that position contradicts the instruction of James 5:14–15 to "call for the elders of the church … and the prayer offered in faith will make the sick person well" (NIV). I saw that it discouraged people from asking or believing for healing, but I also knew that God is over all, not any man.

I determined to trust and obey God as best He made me able. I would preach His promises and invite people to believe them. I resolved to encourage people to go as far as possible in God's direction and see what He would do.

The exercise of faith is simply giving God opportunity to do the impossible. Hebrews 11:1 says, "Faith is the substance of things hoped for, the evidence of things not seen." Things we hope for but cannot see often become a reality when we give God a chance to be God.

We saw it firsthand in Chile. In 1986, my wife, Cherie, and I went with our two sons to San Pedro to conduct a church-planting campaign. The effort began to gain momentum as many people received physical healing. Celmira Cancino's paralyzed arm was healed. Ulfala Hernandez Krauss could not bend her knees but received instant healing. Jose Figueroa was healed of rheumatoid arthritis. Twelve individuals received healing of paralyzed limbs. Twenty-six individuals had deaf ears, but they began to hear after prayer.

One man came to the crusade who had lost almost all use of his left side as the result of a stroke. He walked with great difficulty and could not lift his arm. He came early one Sunday and waited seven hours for prayer. He hobbled up to me when I arrived at the tent for the evening service. I promised I would pray for him but said he should stay for the service and come with the others at the time of prayer for the sick.

After I preached, I prayed first for individuals to accept Christ as Savior. Then I invited those who wanted healing to come forward. The paralyzed man joined about one hundred others who came to the front. When the crowd repeated a simple prayer for healing, some individuals began immediately and loudly to declare they had been healed. From the platform, I looked at the man who had met me before service and told him to try to lift his left arm. He tried without success. I encouraged him to try again. Only his shoulder and body moved when he struggled to lift the arm. I asked him to try yet again, and he raised his arm over his head for the first time in more than a year.

Interestingly, his arm was healed but not his leg. When I invited him to come to the platform, he had difficulty climbing the steps and shuffling over to where I was standing.

"What has the Lord done for you?" I asked him in Spanish.

He said, "He healed my arm!"

Then, to our joy and amazement, when he demonstrated by waving his arm, his paralyzed leg also was healed! It happened so quickly that even he was surprised by his testimony, "He healed my arm *and my leg!*" Then he danced an impromptu jig on the platform to demonstrate and celebrate. The Lord, in His divine timing, had chosen to complete the healing on the platform so the whole crowd could witness a miracle.

What would have happened if the man had not been able to raise his arm after the third challenge? I am not sure. I may have asked him to try again. If he were unable to lift the arm after several efforts, I would have encouraged him to continue believing, continue praising God, and continue coming to the campaign.

I attempted to elevate the man's faith by asking him to raise his arm. We were giving God the opportunity to do the impossible. I cannot claim I knew for certain he was going to be healed. Although many times I have been absolutely convinced a specific individual would be healed when we prayed, most times, it seems, that is not the way divine healing works.

If we only prayed for people when we felt like something was going to happen, we would not pray for many. Instead, we pray for people regardless of how we feel, because we know healing is never our responsibility. Our responsibility, and our blessed privilege, is to offer prayer for the sick and to encourage their faith (James 5:14). *And,* it is our responsibility to trust God with them.

Many miracles occur when Christians simply give God the opportunity to do the impossible. It does not require a supernatural insight or the spiritual "gift of faith," birthing certainty that something phenomenal will take place. God often rewards actions of faith when an individual gives Him a chance.

In the very early days of Christ's church, people came from far and near to seek healing from God. Acts 5:15–16 says, "They brought the sick out into the streets and laid *them* on beds and couches, that at least the shadow of Peter passing by might fall on some of them. Also a multitude gathered from the surrounding cities to Jerusalem, bringing sick people and those who were tormented by unclean spirits, and they were all healed" (NKJV).

What were these believers doing? They were hoping for help and giving God an opportunity to heal. They were taking steps of faith. Obviously, there was no power in Peter's shadow, but they received miracles because they dared to position themselves where God could make a difference.

Hundreds of people have been healed when they responded to a request to do what they had been unable to do before prayer—to bend over if that had been impossible, to breathe deeply if breathing had been their difficulty, etc. In these instances, faith already has been built through preaching of the word of God. A worshipful and expectant atmosphere for miracles has been established. I have seen twisted limbs healed, tumors disappear, deaf ears opened, and blind eyes receive sight, when we simply expected something to happen.

This book offers simple but sound observations to help you receive your own miracle. The explanations are not bizarre or unscriptural. Our guiding principle, our theme, is exercising faith by giving a sovereign God the opportunity to help us.

Man's extremity is God's opportunity, but any kind of need can be an occasion for divine intervention. It should not take desperation to drive us to our heavenly Father. Expectant prayer is our first response, not a last resort. The Apostle Peter wrote, "Give all your worries and cares to God, for he cares about you" 1 Peter 5:6–7 (NLT).

We cannot reduce healing or any answer to prayer to matters of mechanics or formulas; however, there are things we can do and principles we can apply to pave the way. We can pray, exercise faith, and be guided by God's Word. He will respond in His sovereign timing and purpose.

MEET THE HEALER!
A BIBLICAL FOUNDATION

J esus Christ, the Son of God, came to show His Father to the world. He made us know what God is like by demonstrating God's love, mercy, and power. He embodied God's plan for the lost and hurting. Bible scholars might say He is the "exegesis" of God.

The word "exegesis" means proper explanation, interpretation, or exposition. An accurate exegesis of scripture requires the best possible interpretation of any given passage. Certain rules, called hermeneutics, guide the analysis and application. These sets of laws include original grammatical construction and a comparison of how words from the Greek, Hebrew, or Aramaic are used in other locations in the testaments. Good exegesis also involves the historical roots of a passage, the tendencies of the author who wrote the book and cultural implications which influenced idioms, expressions, behavior, etc.

What Bible scholars attempt with correct exegesis is what Jesus did in perfectly revealing the Father. John 1:18 says, "No one has ever seen God. But God the only Son is very close to the Father, and he has shown us what God is like" (New Century Version). The Amplified Bible elaborates on the phrase, "he has shown us what God is like," and offers several shades of meaning: "He has revealed Him and brought Him out where He can be seen; He has interpreted Him and He has made Him known."

Colossians 2:9 says of Jesus Christ that "in Him dwells all the fullness of the Godhead bodily" (NKJV). He told Phillip and His other disciples, "He who has seen Me has seen the Father" (John 14:9, NKJV). He said, "The words I say to you are not just my own. Rather, it is the Father, living in me, who is doing his work" (John 14:10, NIV). Not just His teaching but His life—who He was and all He did—reveal God to us. He told those who challenged His claim to be God's Son, "Do not believe me unless I do what my Father does. But if I do it, even though you do not believe me, believe the miracles, that you may know and understand that the Father is in me, and I in the Father" (John 10:37–39, NIV).

This means that healing the sick was more than a power display. Healing reveals God's nature. It is not just something God does. It is who He is. He is the Healer. In fact, He said so. He told the nation of Israel, "I am the Lord who heals you" (Exodus 15:26, NKJV). Jesus fully expressed God's love and compassion. He spoke God's words and lived out God's purpose. Peter declared, "And no doubt you know that God anointed Jesus of Nazareth with the Holy Spirit and with power. Then Jesus went around doing good and healing all who were oppressed by the Devil, for God was with him" (Acts 10:38, NLT).

Jesus said He came "to seek and to save that which was lost" (Luke 19:10). Matthew shows Christ's approach in His early ministry, "Now Jesus went about all Galilee, teaching in their synagogues, preaching the gospel of the kingdom, and healing all kinds of sickness and all kinds of disease among the people" (Matthew 4:23, KJV). He showed Jesus continuing this pattern throughout His ministry as in Matthew 9:35: "And Jesus went about all the cities and villages, teaching in their synagogues, preaching the gospel of the kingdom, and healing every sickness and every disease among the people."

Wherever Jesus went, He taught, He preached, and He healed the sick. Healing was more than a ministry method; it was part of the message. Charles H. Kraft wrote:

> For Jesus the demonstration of the love of God meant using the power of God as an integral part of his ministry. The "miracles" were a part of the message Jesus lived, not simply a part of the method he used. We cannot, if we properly honor the scriptural revelation, regard his acts of healing and deliverance as secondary to the more intellectual aspects of Jesus's life and ministry. Probably because evangelicals have not experienced this part of our Christian heritage, we tend to see Jesus's miracles more as proofs of his deity than as essential to his message. Yet he himself urged his enemies to focus on his works as proof of his authenticity (John 10:36–38, emphasis added)[2]

Francis MacNutt, in his work titled simply *Healing* argues that "the healing acts of Jesus were themselves the message that He had come to set men free."[3]

Scripture records that those who came to Jesus received healing. Even though He brusquely tested the faith and perseverance of the Canaanite woman who followed Him and begged healing for her daughter, ultimately He commended her faith and granted her request (Matthew 15:22–28; Mark 7:22–30).

The Bible is clear, too, in reporting instances in which Jesus did not heal everyone. He healed "only a few sick folk," in His hometown of Nazareth because of the unbelief of neighbors who thought they knew Him (Matthew 13:54–38). Another time, Jesus healed only one lame man out of the multitudes sprawled around the Pool of Bethesda (John 5:1–14). Nothing suggests this man had greater faith than the rest, or any faith at all. In fact, he did not even know the name of his Healer when pressed to explain why he was carrying his bedroll on the Sabbath.

Jack Deere had this to say concerning the healing of the paralyzed man:

> *The only firm reason for the healing of the paralytic that we can derive from the context of John 5 is that the Father willed it, and Jesus executed His Father's will.... We are ultimately faced with the conclusion that sometimes the Lord works miracles for His own sovereign purposes without giving any explanation for His actions to His followers.*[4]

A sovereign God selected the paralyzed man for a miracle. Why not the others? The answer to that question, if still needed, will only be revealed in eternity.

God's sovereignty is shown again in Acts 3 with the healing of the lame man at the temple gate. The Apostles Peter and John saw the man as they headed to the temple. They looked at him intently, and Peter spoke the classic command: "Silver and gold have I none, but such as I have, I give to you. In the name of Jesus Christ of Nazareth, rise up and walk" (Acts 3:6). Peter seized the man's hand, lifted him up, and instantly his feet and ankles were healed!

This is a display of God's sovereign intervention because the man had been lame since birth, forty years, and he had been placed every day to beg at that same gate (Acts 3:2). Jesus had come to the temple many times, most likely through that very entrance. Jesus had passed him by without a miracle. Why? I can only speculate. Perhaps He reserved this healing for the "greater works" those who believed on Him would do. Whatever the reasons, He did not heal him then, but nothing changes the fact that He healed him afterwards with Peter's command.

He healed the lame man later, after He had risen from the grave and returned to His Father, and after He had empowered His church, His followers, to carry on His work. Later is better than never.

Lazarus learned this when he fell ill and died (John 11). Jesus seemed to ignore the summons of Lazarus' sisters Martha and Mary. He came four days after Lazarus died and He raised him from the tomb. Christ had His own reasons for the delays. At least one seems to be to give God even greater glory than a healing (John 11:40). Of course, Lazarus eventually died again. In fact, everyone Jesus healed died in due course. Healing postponed the inevitable and we always need to make this clear. Healing is not the answer to death: resurrection to eternal life is the sure and final answer.

Postponement can be a good thing. It gave Lazarus a chance to confirm who Jesus was. Many of the Jews believed in Jesus because of Lazarus (John 11:45). The ultimate goal of any healing is to bring glory to Christ and to declare who He is to a sinful generation. A postponement of death gives a greater, extended opportunity to declare it.

We are looking at two great Bible truths. First, "the prayer of faith shall save the sick and God will raise him up" (James 5:15), and, second, God is sovereign. These truths are not in conflict. "Sovereign" does not mean "severe" or "stingy." God rules, and may even overrule, with infinite wisdom, but He is full of compassion and His nature is to give life and to heal. We stand only to gain as we give a sovereign and gracious God every opportunity.

God's ways are higher than ours. We should always pray and believe for healing, even when it does not come immediately. If the postponement of death never comes, for reasons only God can explain, heaven is no defeat.

The fact remains, Jesus does heal and He will continue to heal people who come to Him. He may not always do it immediately, and He may not do it how we expect. In Tonga, a paralyzed lady was brought by her friend who cared for her day and night. The caregiver was healed but not the paralyzed woman. That is not the way I would do it, but I am not God. I have seen paralyzed people healed, but I also have seen some who were not. That does not change my belief in God's healing power nor dampen my expectation of what He will do.

Jesus expected His disciples to do the things He had done on earth. He included all believers in the plan: "He who believes on me, the works that I do he shall do also, and greater works than these he shall do, because I go to my Father" (John 14:12, NKJV). Often scholars are so intent on interpreting the meaning of "greater works" that they miss the point, "He who believes on me, the works that I do he shall do also." Christ made clear these works would continue after He departed, "because I go to my Father." Healing the sick was a part of His "works" or actions on earth. Healing miracles would be continued through those who believed on Him.

The book of Acts chronicles various miracles which occurred with the Apostles, but healings did not cease with them. Stephen was not an Apostle, but he "did great wonders and miraculous signs among the people" (Acts 6:8, NIV). Phillip was not an apostle, but many received healing in his ministry to the Samaritans (Acts 8:6–7). James, half brother to the Lord Jesus, urged the sick, to "call for the elders of the church; and let them pray over him, anointing him with oil in the name of the Lord: And the prayer of faith shall save the sick, and the Lord shall raise him up" (James 5:14–15, NKJV).

The term "elders" refers to mature, spiritual leaders in the church, but all believers can pray for the sick. A passage near the end of the book of Mark says, "These signs will follow those who believe … they will lay hands on the sick and they shall recover" (Mark 16:17–18, NKJV).[5]

Jesus showed us that healing is God's nature, His work, and an integral part of His life-giving message. Through the Holy Spirit, He walks today in the same compassion, showing the love and power of His Father. Jesus Christ has never left His church. He still seeks out men and women who will believe Him for the impossible and trust Him no matter what. He wants us to give Him an opportunity.

Prayer and Miracles

God can do anything He wants and anytime. He may intervene in any life and overrule at will in His creation, but for the most part, He waits for us to ask Him. Prayer cannot be divorced from the miraculous. Philippians 4:6 tells us, "Let your requests be made known to God" (NKJV). Jesus himself said, "Ask and it will be given to you" (Luke 11:19, NIV).

We pray privately and publicly, systematically and spontaneously, inwardly and audibly, but we must be people of prayer if we are to get answers. God's responses do not come because hours of prayer force His hand. Rather, Christ is "touched with the feeling of our infirmities" (Hebrews 4:15, KJV). This, of course, does not minimize the value of spending a lot of time in prayer.

Our priority in praying is getting to know God. He understands us, loves us, and delights in us. The simplest prayer moves Him. The more we understand this, the more we will want to pray and spend time with Him. God longs for us to talk to Him. He wants us to share our problems. Some people are not healed simply because they never pray about their need.

Prayers God Can Answer

Effective, meaningful prayer must begin with believing in the One to whom we pray. Hebrews 11:6 puts it this way, "And without faith it is impossible to please God, because anyone who comes to him must believe that he exists and that he rewards those who earnestly seek him" (NIV). It is all about God, the only God who answers prayer.

When a young man in India was healed of pain in his leg, he told me, "This is the first time any god to whom I prayed has answered my prayers." Our God is powerful and He delights in responding to His servants.

In addition to living faith in the God of heaven, the character and obedience of the one who prays are vital. Mighty demonstrations of God's power call for a life of obedience. Prayer from the lips of an individual striving to line up and live up to God's Word is most powerful.

The New Testament writer James instructed: "Confess your sins to each other and pray for each other so that you may be healed. The prayer of a righteous man is powerful and effective" (James 5:16, NIV). The context of this Bible verse—what comes before and after—shows that potent and productive prayer follows being forthright with fellow believers. The righteous person does not allow pretense to hinder prayer. "Righteous" means "in right standing with God through faith in His Son, Jesus Christ."

The Amplified Bible draws deeper shades of meaning from the original Greek of James 5:16:

> *Confess to one another therefore your faults (your slips, your false steps, your offenses, your sins) and pray [also] for one another, that you may be healed and restored*

[to a spiritual tone of mind and heart]. The earnest (heartfelt, continued) prayer of a righteous man makes tremendous power available [dynamic in its working].

The praying person must be earnest, praying from the heart. He or she must faithfully practice regular and frequent prayer. He must be obedient and holy. When all of this falls into place, tremendous power comes into play.

This is not to suggest that only perfect people get answers from God. It is to help us better to know how to access the dynamic power available through prayer. Candor about our false steps and failures can clear the way for healing and restoration at every level.

The Apostle John added this encouragement in 1 John 3:22: "And whatsoever we ask, we receive of him, because we keep his commandments, and do those things that are pleasing in his sight (KJV)" Nothing gives a believer more confidence in prayer than living in obedience to God's Word. Exposing every area of our lives, even the deepest, secret places to the penetrating impact of the Scriptures generates powerful praying.

For the word of God is full of living power. It is sharper than the sharpest knife, cutting deep into our innermost thoughts and desires. It exposes us for what we really are. Nothing in all creation can hide from God. Everything is naked and exposed before His eyes. This is the God to whom we must explain all that we have done. That is why we have a great High Priest who has gone to heaven, Jesus, the Son of God. Let us cling to Him and never stop trusting Him. This High Priest of ours understands our weaknesses, for He faced all of the same temptations we do, yet He did not sin. So let us come boldly to the throne of our gracious God. There we will receive his mercy, and we will find grace to help us when we need it (Hebrews 4:12–16, NLT).

The Word of God cuts deep and precise to expose our private thoughts and motives. It shows who and what we really are. When we call on God, He already knows our hearts. This should move us to total honesty when we pray. The truly righteous person sees, even in himself, what God sees.

Unconfessed sin blocks the prayer life. You may sing, lead public prayer, or even preach while ignoring sin in your life, but you cannot pray effectively, if at all, when you are alone with God. King David said, "If I had not confessed the sin in my heart, my Lord would not have listened. But God did listen! He paid attention to my prayer" (Psalm 66:18, NLT). After David confessed his sin, God listened. We must deal with sin as God sees it, confess it, and forsake it. Then refuse to live in condemnation after seeking His forgiveness (Romans 8:1).

Thank God for our High Priest! We cling to Him and always trust Him. We never come on our own merits and we do not deserve His favor. We are accepted because of who He is and what He has done. We willingly and constantly let him search our hearts, because He is the God of grace. We come boldly to Him, knowing He looks on us with pleasure.

FAITH AND MIRACLES

Prayer and faith are mutually dependent. Prayer is the primary vehicle for expressing and beginning to exercise faith. But prayer without faith in God does not get results. Jesus warned against empty prayers voiced just to be heard of others (Luke 20:47).

A small placard on our wall when I was growing up said, "Prayer Changes Things." Does it really? Prayer alone does not bring change. If so, then Hindus, Buddhists, and Muslims would change the world. They often are more devoted to prayer than Christians. Prayer that moves God, that draws His response, must be combined with faith in Him as the only living, sovereign God. Jesus expected His followers to believe for answers whenever they prayed. He said, "Whatever you ask for in prayer, believe that you have received it, and it will be yours" Mark. 11:24 (NIV).

How Do I Pray in Faith?

Believing prayer must be in keeping with God's Word. To pray contrary to what the Bible tells us cancels the possibility of a positive answer. When we base our petitions on what God has promised, we can make our requests with confidence. The Apostle Paul said of Christ, "In him and through faith in him, we may approach God with freedom and confidence" (Ephesians 3:12, NIV). One of the Lord's original twelve disciples, John, said, "This is the confidence we have in approaching God: that if we ask anything according to his will, he hears us. And if we know that he hears us whatever we ask we know that we have what we asked of him" (1 John 5:14–15, NIV).

Faith does not depend on feelings. It stands in the certainty of who God is (Hebrews 11:6). Wonderful feelings may follow faith, especially when it is boldly confessed and demonstrated, but believing God and having Him answer our prayers is not a matter of how we feel. Faith rests in Christ alone and, if necessary, waits for His answer.

Soon after I started preaching and traveling as an evangelist, I was praying one Sunday afternoon for the final service of an extended meeting. I concentrated on the service as I paced and prayed in the church sanctuary, but my immediate financial need also came to mind. I needed a certain amount in the final offering. I did not dwell on the need, but I included it in my prayer and asked the Lord for the specific amount.

That night the pastor did something unusual when he received the offering. The pans had been passed but the gifts not tallied when he said, "I feel like we need ten more dollars" (Now you know for sure that this was *many* years ago). Different individuals contributed a dollar or two, and the offering was completed. When the pastor gave it to me, it counted out to exactly what I needed and had mentioned in prayer.

I was amazed—not that the Lord had provided exactly what I needed. He had done that before. I was amazed that

I had to do no more than mention the need to God. I had not spent the afternoon trying to make sure I got an answer. I did not have to pray until I felt good about the situation. No revelation came to me. I simply asked and simple faith proved more powerful than I realized. It seemed the ten dollars postscript had been added just to let me know, and to reaffirm for the pastor and the people, that God keeps perfect records. He knows just when and how to intervene.

The amounts needed for campaign expenses and building projects around the world have grown exponentially through the years, but God has not changed. He still is bigger than all creation. Praying faithfully and fervently builds discipline and faith grows. Believing is not so hard when God has answered so many times. It starts with something like the direct answer I received those many years ago.

As a word of caution, we should never limit God by expecting Him always to do things the same way. He is a God of infinite variety, and we must give Him room to be God. He will choose the vehicle to deliver your miracle. Couple your prayer with faith, active assurance, and trust in Him, as He has revealed Himself in His Word.

PRAYING WITH AUTHORITY

Most Christians do not pray with authority. Some who do take on a spiritual cockiness that implies God is their servant instead of the other way around. We need biblical balance, but we must learn to be authoritative in our praying. Prayer is not begging God for an answer. Christ gives authority to believers and expects us to use it. If we pray for healing, we have no reason to be timid in embracing God's promises.

Jesus told His disciples, "All authority in heaven and on earth has been given to me" (Matthew 28:18, NIV). He taught them to use that authority when he insisted, "I tell you the truth, anyone who has faith in me will do what I have been doing" (John. 14:12, NIV). If we are to do what Jesus did, it is wise to study how He did it. He said to the man at the pool of Bethesda, "Get up! Pick up your mat and walk!" (John 5:8). He gave basically the same charge to another paralytic in Matthew 9:7: "Get up, take your mat and go home!" (NIV). The verses that follow say, "The man got up and went home. When the crowd saw this, they were filled with awe; and they praised God, who had given such authority to men" (Matthew 9:7–8, NIV). The crowds clearly recognized divine authority at work.

Christ's disciples were faithful to follow His orders. They carried on in His authority. In Acts 3, Peter commanded a lame man to be healed. In Acts 9:34, he ordered Aeneas, who had been in bed for eight years, to get up and make his bed. Again, he spoke to the lifeless body of the seamstress in Acts 9:40, "Tabitha, get up." Peter spoke forcefully each time, using the powerful name of Jesus. In fact, this shows something of what it means to pray, preach, teach, baptize, and do whatever in word or deed "in the name of Jesus" (Acts 9:27; Colossians 3:17).

Our authority comes from praying in agreement with the Word and the will of God. We do not pray in our own name or out of our own ability. I often quote the Word of God, our supreme authority, in praying for the sick. A bold faith declaration or an authoritative instruction gives God an opportunity to work a miracle.

"Get Out Of That Bed!"

I saw this proved in San Lorenzo, Paraguay. One night after a church planting campaign service, a young lady who had been saved in the meetings asked me to come to her house to pray for her father. I took the pastor and his wife, and we followed the young lady to her home. I could sense demonic presence when we entered the house, and I learned later that the young lady's mother was a *bruja* (witch) who studied and practiced witchcraft.

The young woman led us to the back bedroom where her father lay in bed. The man could not move his legs and could hardly speak above a whisper. He was very bitter about his situation and really was not happy we had come. I talked to him briefly about his need to repent of his sins and he prayed a sinner's prayer to accept the Lord Jesus as His Savior. Then I had him repeat a prayer for his healing.

While I was praying, doubt crept into my mind. I thought I probably should not try to get the man out of bed. "After all," I reasoned, or perhaps Satan whispered, "God doesn't always heal everyone instantly." When I said the "amen" to our prayer, I did not have time to say anything else. The pastor's wife, standing behind me, shouted out with authority, "Get out of that bed and walk in the name of Jesus!" The man immediately got up and began to walk. At the same time, his voice was restored! God saw to it that someone would take authority over Satan, and the man was healed.

This experience helped me determine to use that kind of authority to give God opportunities to do the impossible. It is true that not every person I pray for gets out of the wheelchair or starts seeing immediately from blind eyes, but I still am responsible to give God specific opportunities to work. Not everyone is healed, but some are. And that drives me to keep on praying and speaking to the hurting in the name of Jesus.

Now I instruct the sick after prayer, "Try to do what you could not do before, in the name of Jesus! Bend over, in Jesus's name! Walk, in Jesus's name! Move a finger, in the name of Jesus! Test your eyesight, in Jesus's name!" Many times it is necessary to rebuke doubt, unbelief and demonic power in the same breath. We must exercise God's authority over spiritual powers and physical afflictions. Satan is no match for a Holy Spirit-empowered vessel. The one inside us still is greater than he who is in the world, Satan (1 John 4:4). Praise God!

Praying Out Loud

God responds to faith-filled prayer without regard to volume. Prayer may be silent, it may be loud, or anywhere in between. An old adage says, "God is not deaf, but neither is He nervous!" The Psalmist said, "Let the words of my mouth and the meditation of my heart be acceptable in your sight O Lord, my strength and my redeemer" (Psalms 19:14, NKJV). Both the spoken and meditated word can be acceptable to God.

Occasionally, time and situation permit only a thought directed to God. When Nehemiah the cupbearer for King Artaxerxes, was burdened by the devastation of Jerusalem, the king asked him why he was sad (Nehemiah. 2:1–5). Nehemiah told him about the city of his ancestors, and the king asked, "How can I help?" Though Nehemiah may have been surprised by the royal offer, he did not waste the opportunity. He sent up a silent prayer before he outlined a rebuilding plan for the king. Nehemiah did not run outside to pray or drop to his knees and cry aloud. He prayed with his thoughts.

Just as volume alone is not an issue in prayer, God does not give extra credit for posture. Kneeling may reflect humility. Falling on our faces may speak of surrender and worship. Walking may help animate our petitions, but our posture when we pray has no bearing on the outcome. The position of the heart not the body is what matters. Some may not be able to stand, walk, or kneel. Sitting or lying in bed is their only option, and God still answers their prayers.

It is important to understand that prayer posture and volume cannot be prescribed; however, we still can find value in praying different ways. Some people never vocalize their prayers. They need to try it. Hearing ourselves pray can help us become more expressive. Do not limit your praying to silent meditation. Sounding out your praise and requests can elevate your faith and inspire others. Many times praying aloud helps keep focus on our prayer objectives and minimizes distractions.

Learn to pray for people out loud. Learn to pray out loud in private devotions. Learn to serve notice on Satan that he is defeated. Take a cue from Michael the archangel when he said to Satan, "The Lord rebuke you!" (Jude 9; Zechariah 3:2).[6]

When I was young, I attended a church where no one ever prayed aloud except the preacher or someone he designated. My first service in a Pentecostal church seemed very strange with the whole church praying and praising out loud, and at the same time! Not only did I become accustomed to this biblical practice, I grew very comfortable with praying out loud in my private times of seeking the Lord.

The Bible both allows and encourages audible prayer. David said, "As for me, I will call upon God, and the LORD shall save me. Evening and morning and at noon I will pray, and cry aloud, and He shall hear my voice" (Psalm 55:16–17, NKJV). Some versions render "cry aloud" as "cry out in distress" (NIV) and others as a complaint and moaning (RSV) but the end of the verse always remains the same, "He shall hear *my voice*" (emphasis added). In another psalm, David said, "I cry aloud to the LORD; I lift up my voice to the LORD for mercy. I pour out my complaint before him; before him I tell my trouble" (Psalm 142:1–2, NIV). He clearly felt comfortable hearing himself and being heard praying.

Praying together and praying out loud never are discouraged in the Scripture. An impressive list of Bible heroes prayed out loud (It would have been hard otherwise to record their prayers.) The catalog includes Jacob (Genesis 32:9); Moses (Deuteronomy 9:26); Samson (Judges 6:28); David (2 Samuel 15:31); Elijah (1 Kings 18:36); Hezekiah (2 Kings 19:15); Nehemiah (Nehemiah 6:9); Jonah (Jonah 2:1–9); Jesus (Matthew 26:39, John 17); Stephen (Acts 7:59); and others.

The early church prayed together and they prayed aloud. "They raised their voices together in prayer to God" (Acts 4:24, NIV). God responded mightily to their united prayer: "After they prayed, the place where they were meeting was shaken. And they were all filled with the Holy Spirit and spoke the word of God boldly" (Acts 4:31, NIV). God had no difficulty sorting out their petitions and answering every one.

However you express them, pray effective, believing prayers. When the pastor or leader asks the congregation to join in prayer, he doesn't mean just listen. Pray with him. Believe with him. Lift up your voice with others when the opportunity to pray is given. Link your faith with other believers and prepare for God's answer. Healing and miracles happen when God's people pray.

PRACTICING THE PRESENCE
(BUILDING A RELATIONSHIP WITH GOD)

Walking with God is more than dutiful obedience; it is a growing relationship. Every believer should move beyond the initial elements of Christian experience—the foundation of repentance, saving faith, and core Christian doctrines—to pursue a lifetime of growing closer to and becoming more like Jesus. The result of walking closely with Him, communing in prayer and study of His Word, is ever increasing faith.

The writer of Hebrews catalogs Old Testament heroes who believed God (Hebrews 11) before focusing on Jesus as the source and means of faith. Believers are to run the race of life "looking unto Jesus, the author and finisher of our faith" (Hebrews 12:2, KJV). In the original Greek of the text, the word *aphorao* translated "looking" means "intently gazing." The word for *author* means "initiator" and the word rendered *finisher* in the King James Version means "perfecter."

Richard Weymouth's translation makes the phrase read, "simply fixing our gaze upon Jesus, the Leader and Perfecter of faith." Christ initiates faith and carries it to completion as we follow Him. It comes with being in His presence, "intently gazing," keeping Him the center of our focus.

We should want supernatural faith, but our real goal is Christ Himself. We do not come into His presence to ask for faith. We come in order to know Him. The better we know Him, the better we trust Him, the more we believe. He perfects our faith.

Help My Unbelief?

What about the man who asked Jesus to "help his unbelief"? Didn't he pray for faith? The man in Mark 9 came to Jesus with his demon harassed son after the disciples had failed to help him. He said, "If you can do anything, take pity on us and help us" (Mark.9:22, NIV). Jesus's reply in the New International Version of the New Testament repeats the man's statement as a question, "'If you can'?' said Jesus. 'Everything is possible for him who believes'" (Mark 9:23, NIV). He gave the father a responsibility to believe and the man cried in desperation, "I do believe; help me overcome my unbelief!" (Mark 9:24, NIV).

Just a moment in the presence of Jesus brought this man to realize his bankruptcy of faith. He pleaded for whatever it would take to set his son free. He was willing to believe. Christ restored the son completely, not because of the father's great faith, but because of who He is. Whatever faith the father had, he placed it all in Jesus. That is the key! Even a little faith in a big God can trigger a miracle.

Like the father in the story, we understand Christ is the only miracle worker. We have the responsibility to believe, but, unlike the father meeting Jesus for the first time, we have opportunity to practice the presence. That is, we can constantly acknowledge Him in attitude and talk to Him in all opportune moments. Even the original disciples who physically walked with Jesus had to learn the value of fervent, frequent prayer in order to see God meet such desperate needs (Mark. 11:28–29, NIV). When we practice His presence, faith grows out of who Christ is rather than who we are. His faith works in us, not just because we imitate Him, but because He lives in and through us. We take on His character.

The Veil and the Mirror

The Apostle Paul said, "We all, with unveiled face, beholding as in a mirror the glory of the Lord, are being transformed into the same image from glory to glory, just as by the Spirit of the Lord" (2 Corinthians. 3:18, NKJV). This passage likens the veil over Moses' face after being in the divine presence to the cloak over the hearts of Jews of Paul's day who could not accept the risen Christ as God's Son. In contrast, we who know the Lord Jesus Christ as Savior, come to Him in prayer and devotion with nothing between us. We see more and more who He is and the Holy Spirit changes us to be more and more like Him. We begin to reflect Him to others.

Paul compares us to a mirror. A mirror does not have to work to produce an image. That is by nature what a mirror does. Likewise, our new nature reflects Him who lives in us. We do not fake faith. We have it because we spend time in His presence. Spending time in His presence, we go from "glory to glory."

Unlike the glory Moses experienced in the Old Testament, the glory of Christ does not fade. It increases!

His glory will never fade. We only fail to reflect Him, and miss what He wants us to experience, when we pull away from or neglect times in His presence.

Believe to See His Glory

What is the glory of God? Here is a working definition: *It is radiance and power often demonstrated by the miraculous but which does not have to be manifested to be inherently true of God.* There are at least two aspects of God's glory. One is inherent, who God is—all powerful, all knowing, all loving, pure, perfect, and just—no matter what anyone does or believes. He is God all by Himself! The other is manifest glory as God makes Himself known by action or expression. The Lord taught me one wonderful night that we can believe for a manifestation of His glory.

I was seated on an outdoor platform in Coimbatore, India, waiting to preach to about two thousand people. As I listened to the inspired singing, I began to feel impressed with the Lord's statement to Martha at the tomb of her brother Lazarus, "Did I not say to you that if you would believe you would see the glory of God?" (John 11:40, NKJV). I realized this was to be my topic that night rather than the sermon I had prepared. Deep inside, I became aware of something that I had not understood about God. We could believe to see His glory! I knew God can and does manifest His glory at His pleasure, but I began to realize He also wants us to believe to see His glory.

I had no neatly typed pages or even hand-scribbled notes. The thoughts about God's glory flowed as I preached. I told of men who saw the glory of God. There was the Prophet Isaiah who saw God's glory in the temple

(Isaiah 6:1–10). God initiated this manifestation to commission the prophet to a new level of ministry. Moses, on the other hand, requested that he might see God's glory (Exodus 33:18). God responded by letting him see as much as a human could survive.

In Martha's case, the glory of God was connected to an incredible miracle. Jesus raised her brother from the dead after four days in the tomb! (John 11:38–44). I understood, for the first time that night in India, that if we somehow could be in God's presence and believe specifically for His glory, incredible miracles would happen.

What followed the preaching was a very powerful demonstration of God's power. Some threw away crutches, and others were healed of deafness, blindness, and any number of diseases. One young man from the United States said he had never seen anything like it except on television. God revealed Himself in response to a crowd of people who believed to see His glory.

The lesson I brought home from India was that we too often pray to see God's power instead of His glory. We ask for miracles, not His glory. Our ultimate goal must be to see Him not just gain from His power. Even with answered prayer, the miracle is not complete until God gets all the glory. When we want Christ and Christ alone, faith comes.

Internalizing the Word

A key to practicing God's presence and unlocking the miraculous is internalizing His Word. *Internalize* means *to adopt the beliefs, values, and attitudes of others, consciously or unconsciously.* It means taking in those thoughts, principles, and practices until they become our own. We do this in a divine dimension when we fill ourselves with the Word of God. We take it in by every means—read it, hear it, study it, memorize it, and meditate on it. We make it saturate our thoughts and actions.

Jesus said, "If you abide in me, and my words abide in you, you will ask what you desire, and it shall be done for you" (John. 15:7, NKJV). Between relationship and answered prayer, our Lord sandwiched the need to cling to what He said. The promise came as he emphasized to his disciples the necessity of abiding or remaining in a healthy, living relationship with Him as the true vine.

In the four Bible books he wrote, John uses the word *abide* ("remain" in some translations) fourteen times. Seven of them appear in just five verses (John 15:4–7, 10). Branches, or disciples, who abide in the vine will bear much fruit. Branches which remain fruitless because they have no source or flow of life will lose out.

Thank God the words of Christ are recorded and the New Testament is complete. Believers today have the advantage of daily study and modern technology multiplies how we can do it. We have the word in myriad translations on our computers and handheld devices. We have audio and video versions. He also uses the proclaimed message of the Word to build our faith.

Romans 10:17 says, "Faith comes by hearing and hearing by the word of God" (NKJV). Paul makes it contextually obvious that this means hearing the preached word of God with understanding and application.[7] In previous verses in this chapter, Paul, the author of Romans, had answered questions about the Jewish people who had not accepted Christ. He explained that salvation comes when you "confess with your mouth the Lord Jesus and believe in your heart that God has raised Him from the dead" (Romans 10:9, NKJV). The most basic promise of God, His promise to save through faith in His Son, must be taken to heart.

The Word abiding or remaining in us produces the necessary faith to receive from God and to keep negative concepts or actions from neutralizing His work. The Psalmist David declared, "Thy word have I hid in mine heart that I might not sin against thee" (Psalms 119:11, KJV). He knew the power of God's Word inside is the greatest deterrent to wrong conduct.

The Apostle Peter described the impact of God's Word in us.

His divine power has given us everything we need for life and godliness through our knowledge of him who called us by his own glory and goodness. [4] Through these he has given us his very great and precious promises, so that through them you may participate in the divine nature and escape the corruption in the world caused by evil desires. (2 Peter 1:3–4 NIV)

The King James Version says "partakers of the divine nature." The New Living Translation says, "share in his divine nature." The original Greek for "partakers" means "become partners." We take on not the quality that makes Him God, but his character of purity and holiness. We become more like Jesus by taking in God's Word.

The common denominator in these proclamations of David and Peter is the power of the Word of God. This transforming Word is available to all believers but not everyone has obeyed the Scripture, "Be diligent to present yourself approved to God, a worker who does not need to be ashamed, rightly dividing the word of truth" (2 Timothy 2:15, NKJV). God's promises work in us more and more as we internalize them, meditate on them, memorize them, and believe them based on an accurate understanding of their context.

His nature comes alive in us through our close association with Him and our knowledge of His Word. When we pray, we believe because we know something of how great God is. We know nothing is impossible for Him. We know He never has forbidden us to ask largely of Him. When an answer does not come in an instant or does not arrive in the way we expected, we refuse to be discouraged. Because we focus on the giver not the gift, our confidence does not shatter.

We know whom we serve! Not just about Him, we know Him! We know who He is. We know His word, His works, and His ways. His ways are ways of love and power. His words are words of promise and purpose. We take them in. We live them out. He lives in us. We live in Him. Walking with Him in this kind of relationship creates and maintains an atmosphere where extraordinary things can happen.

Memorizing and internalizing the promises of an eternal God who cannot lie (Titus 1:2) inspires us to new levels of faith. We move beyond merely acknowledging or conceding that God is all-powerful to an absolute confidence. Knowing His Word this way puts a tool in our hands to resist doubt and correctly appropriate the promises of God.

A Child with Polio Healed

As missions director for Southwestern Assemblies of God University, I took teams of students each year to help start churches in other countries. Our first group from SAGU went to Mexico in 1992. The daily regimen during the trip emphasized memorizing scripture and prayer. We prayed for an hour each day then went to the streets and from house to house to build relationships, invite people to the campaign, tell everyone we could about Jesus, and pray for anyone who desired.

During prayer time before going to the streets, one student, Paul Alexander, began to pray the scriptures he had memorized. Faith began to build inside him as he recited those promises to God.

When the students went out, Paul and the two girls on his team saw a woman get off a bus with her three-year-old grandson in her arms. She recognized them because she had attended the campaign, and she signaled for them to come to her. She sobbed as she told them she had just returned from the doctor with bad news. Her grandson had polio and would never walk again.

Immediately, the scriptures he had been quoting in prayer came rushing to Paul's mind and triggered great faith in his spirit. He shared the same scriptures with the woman and the team prayed for her. They went home with her and spent the morning praying and giving her assurance.

When they returned, Paul ran to report to me what was happening. He said, "I just know that boy is going to be healed." Sure enough the grandmother brought him that night and he had already been healed. He could walk! He was still clinging to her and crying but the next night he was running all over the place.

Paul Alexander's (now Dr. Alexander—he earned his PhD several years later) experience has been repeated many times in the lives of students and others I have known. Internalizing the Word helps us to grasp how God views a situation. That Word inside us can spring to life to meet any given challenge.

Praying the Word

Something in God's book addresses your need. When you pray the Word and according to His Word, you are praying in His will. Acts 4:21–30 shows the church praying the Scriptures:

And being let go, they went to their own companions and reported all that the chief priests and elders had said to them. So when they heard that, they raised their voice to God with one accord and said: "Lord, You are God, who made heaven and earth and the sea, and all that is in them, who by the mouth of Your servant David have said:

"'Why did the nations rage,

And the people plot vain things?

The kings of the earth took their stand,

And the rulers were gathered together

Against the Lord and against His Christ."

For truly against Your holy Servant Jesus, whom You anointed, both Herod and Pontius Pilate, with the Gentiles and the people of Israel, were gathered together to do whatever Your hand and Your purpose determined before to be done. Now, Lord, look on their threats, and grant to Your servants that with all boldness they may speak Your word, by stretching out Your hand to heal, and that signs and wonders may be done through the name of Your holy Servant Jesus (NKJV).

God had worked a miracle through Peter and John by healing a lame man at the Temple Gate (Acts 3:1–10). The religious authorities had arrested them and ordered them to stop preaching and teaching in the name of Jesus. Instead, the Apostles rushed to their fellow believers and they all prayed. They started by establishing the most important fact in every situation, "Lord, you are God!" They recognized Him as the maker of everything and stacked their problems against the backdrop of His power.

Next, they recalled what He had said. Unfolding circumstances did not catch God off guard. He already had spoken what they needed to know and He still was in control. Because they knew His Word, they knew the outcome! Ultimately, they would prevail.

They related God's promise to their situation, "Now, Lord, look on their threats." When you pray according to God's Word, your problem is His problem. Finally, they reached out to God for more of His glory, "Grant to Your servants that with all boldness they may speak Your word, by stretching out Your hand to heal, and that signs and wonders may be done through the name of Your holy Servant Jesus."

Then they received His powerful answer, "And when they had prayed, the place where they were assembled together was shaken; and they were all filled with the Holy

Spirit, and they spoke the word of God with boldness" (Acts 4:31, NKJV).

Using the Scriptures Correctly

The better we know the Word of God, the more effective we become in praying and believing. This does *not* mean lifting scriptures out of their context to suit our fancies. Everything in the Bible means only what is dictated by its context. We cannot claim what God has not promised. A haphazard, wishful thinking approach to the Word can lead to disappointment, frustration, and, even injured faith.

A man interested in a woman who does not reciprocate the interest may quote God's words for months from Genesis 2:24, "they shall be one flesh" (KJV). He may expect a miracle of matrimony, but he ought not be surprised if he still meets rejection. The whole verse says, "Therefore shall a man leave his father and his mother, and shall cleave unto his wife: and they shall be one flesh" (KJV). It speaks of a union already decided and emphasizes the necessary impact on family relationships. It has nothing to do with what one party or another may hope about marriage. In fact, when it comes to the will of another individual, no amount of scripture confessing and promise quoting is guaranteed to make the target change.

When we understand the intention of our Sovereign God, we have confidence in what He has promised. The Apostle John wrote to believers about eternal life through Christ:

> *This is the confidence that we have in approaching*
> *God: that if we ask anything according to his will, he*

hears us. And if we know that he hears us——whatever
we ask—we know that we have what we asked of him
(John 5:14–15 NIV)

This incredible promise should give all believers boldness to declare that they know they are children of God because they have asked Him for eternal life.

This kind of confidence can carry over when we ask for healing, based on the promises of healing in the Word of God. New Testament writer James said, "And the prayer offered in faith will make the sick person well, the Lord will raise him up" (James 5:15, NIV). We pray boldly for the sick, confidently expecting them to be healed, because that is what the scriptures teach us to do. Our prayer of faith is rooted in the Word, even when answers do not immediately follow. Later in this book, we will deal with the fact some may not be healed and why that should not diminish our faith.

The basic lesson about faith and the Word is that God honors what He said. His promises are an antidote to the viruses of doubt and unbelief. It is vital that we know God's Word for faith to take root. In His wilderness temptation, Christ countered every challenge from the devil with, "It is written" (Matthew 4:4, 7, 10, KJV). Even when the enemy misused God's Word, Jesus stifled him with, "It is written again …" (Matthew 4:7, KJV), and he set the record straight. He gave us a powerful pattern.

CHANGING THE CLIMATE OF UNBELIEF—FAITH ENCOUNTERS

Faith cannot rest only on experience. What we believe must be based upon God's word, but seeing Him meet needs can ignite faith in His promises and power. It can serve as a powerful catalyst for giving God an opportunity. Witnessing a miracle can be a stepping stone to greater things as long as we keep our focus on the miracle giver.

The Bible gives many examples of one person's healing or miracle sparking faith in others. After Jesus healed a leper, he "could no longer openly enter the city but was outside in deserted places; and they came to Him from every direction" (Mark 1:45, NKJV). He had told the leper not to tell anyone but he could not keep quiet. As a result, many came to Jesus expecting to be healed. He could not even enter the city because of the crowds.

When Paul the Apostle was shipwrecked on the island of Malta, he was welcomed into the home of Publius, the chief official (Acts 28:7, NIV). Publius's father was suffering from fever and dysentery but when Paul prayed for him and laid his hands on him, the man was healed (Acts 28:8). As a result, "The rest of those on the island who had diseases also came and were healed" (Acts 28:9, NKJV). Their faith was stirred by what happened to the father of their chief official.

Many Christians never place themselves in a position to see a miracle. Some have been taught that healing or other supernatural manifestations do not come in response to prayer. Others minimize their own faith and mistakenly decide God would never do it for them. Still others, and this may be the most tragic circumstance, attend churches which seldom give God an opportunity to do the impossible.

This may be true even in churches whose doctrinal statements include healing. They preach no sermons on healing. They do not pray for healing, and they do not see people healed. The atmosphere does not cultivate faith. They are like Jesus's hometown. No doubt good people were there but Matthew records, "He did not many mighty works there because of their unbelief" (Matthew 13:58, KJV).

A Miracle in Quito

A woman in Quito, Ecuador attended a church like that for twenty-seven years. She said she never heard a sermon on healing, though she suffered almost unbearable arthritis pain. She came to our outdoor campaign in 1985. In fact, our tent was set up on the lot beside her house. We connected to her electricity because the electric company had not installed our meter for the first service. She was a Christian and had prayed for a "Christian campaign, not a circus" when she saw the tent going up.

She came to the service that night, and each night. Her knees were so swollen she could hardly walk. After three nights, she asked to say something to the crowd. She said the swelling had disappeared and her knees no longer were sore. She had received miraculous healing as she worshiped and heard the Word.

Ironically, the church she attended was affiliated with a 100-year-old denomination whose founder made healing a doctrinal cornerstone. As time passed, the healing message was de-emphasized or neglected to the point it is seldom, if ever, mentioned.

The woman healed in the campaign well may have received her miracle sooner, had she heard a faith building message on Christ's power to heal. Instead, she had a miracle on hold. After she was healed, she became a woman of great faith. She believed for others to be healed and came to expect the impossible. Her faith grew as she watched others receive from God. The more we see God do, the more confident we become that He will do it again.

Even when we pray and nothing seems to happen, it does not dampen our faith. It reminds us He is in charge. How and when He responds are in His hands, but the more we learn about Him, the more we want to trust Him.

Changing the Climate of Unbelief

Sometimes just one miracle or one dynamic testimony can change the whole climate of unbelief. Early in our ministry, my wife, Cherie, and I started a church in Managua, Nicaragua. God gave outstanding miracles in the nightly services. Daily radio programs and occasional telecasts helped advertise what was happening.

Manuel Bonilla, a restaurant owner in the nearby town of Tipi Tapa, heard us while he was driving. At first, he was aggravated that a religious broadcast had replaced his usual programs. Though he changed stations at first, eventually he stayed tuned and as he listened to the testimonies each day, he thought of his wife Francis, at home in bed.

Señora Bonilla had a paralyzed arm and wore braces on her neck and back. She survived on thirty different injections and pills each day and needed help with bathing and the most basic tasks. She could not stand noise because of the vicious headaches it produced. According to her doctors, Francis did not have long to live.

After listening for a few days, Manuel rushed into Francis's room and began to tell her about the miracles taking place. Without thinking, he clicked on the television and, at that moment, our first telecast was being aired. Francis normally could not endure the pain from the TV noise, but she watched that afternoon with keen interest. In a weak voice, she said to her husband, "I want to go to that."

Manuel brought Francis to the campaign, but she was too weak to leave the car. She listened to the service from the backseat. Periodically, he asked if she needed to go home. Repeatedly, she said, "No, I want to listen." They stayed to the end and Francis, from the back of the car, repeated the prayer for salvation and then a prayer for healing.

On the way home, Manuel asked whether she felt any better. She responded, "No, but I want to come back."

They continued to come, but Francis still could not get out of the car.

On the third night, Manuel repeated the question he had asked every night on the way home, "Do you feel any better?"

This time her answer was a weak, "I feel a little better."

They kept coming until one night Francis came to the platform to testify of her healing. No one would have guessed her previous condition. Her arm no longer was paralyzed. The braces were gone. She no longer needed pills and she testified that despite twenty-five years as a chain smoker, all desire for cigarettes was gone!

Cherie and I spent an afternoon with the Bonillas at their restaurant where they detailed what God had done for them. Relatives who had come to pay their last respects to Francis before she died were astounded to see her in perfect health. She radiated the joy of the Lord as she shared on our next telecast the wonderful things God had done.

The testimonies of others contributed to Francis's faith. The telecast they viewed included a five-year-old girl who had polio and could not walk before prayer. God had made her well. Others also demonstrated what God had done for them, sparking faith and hope in the Bonillas. In turn, the dramatic change in Francis triggered faith in others.

In August 2010, Cherie and I returned to Nicaragua for another church-building campaign. We had the privilege of ministering again in the church which sprang from the meetings Francis attended. The handful of people worshiping in the open air campaign has grown into a church family twenty-five thousand strong and meeting for six services each Sunday in spacious facilities. Faith encounters are continuing to generate faith.

Even reading stories of miracles can contribute to our faith. People who are praying for divine intervention should study the miracles of healing found in the gospels and the book of Acts. Matthew 8 and 9 are two great chapters which focus on the miracles of Christ.

Faith also is enriched by studying God's work in the lives of individuals of great faith such as Smith Wigglesworth, John G. Lake, Kathryn Kuhlman and others. However, nothing except the Bible bolsters our faith more than when God touches us personally with a miracle. A past blessing advances us in a current challenge.

Churches need miracles. When God confirms His Word with supernatural signs, people come to Christ and the suffering is delivered. Those who never give God an opportunity miss the domino impact on families when a loved one is healed or set free. Nothing encourages a congregation like undeniable miracles and witnessing the handiwork of their God, who delights in the impossible.

If you never have experienced that kind of miracle, get ready! Anything can happen when you give God the opportunity!

Asking Again and Again

Ask and keep on asking God to meet your needs. Expect and keep on expecting Him to answer. Practicing these biblical principles vitally relates to praying in faith. True faith will be persistent. This means more than empty repetitions or recitation of mechanical formulas. It means to pray fervently and frequently in anticipation until there no longer is a need.

In my first church-planting mission many years ago in Asuncion, Paraguay, I emphasized the power of Christ to heal. Every night for two months, a man and his wife carried their paralyzed three-year-old daughter into the services. Night after night, they heard a message on faith, salvation, and healing. Night after night, they prayed she would be able to walk, but nothing seemed to happen.

They kept coming until one night they arrived almost too excited to talk. They brought their daughter forward, and she ran across the platform as if nothing ever had been wrong!

Something wonderful happened within the twenty-four hours from service to service, but it came after two months of faithful attendance and fervent petition. Today that little girl is a married woman with adult children and grandchildren of her own. She is still healed and still serving God in the church that was planted. The miracle that changed all of their lives came because her parents were persistent.

Determined Faith Keeps on Asking

Persistence is the quality or action of continuing steadily despite problems or difficulties. In spiritual things, it is a determined faith which keeps on seeking God with tenacity and resolve. This does not mean we need to wear down God's resistance. It is simply refusing to be distracted or discouraged if the answer is delayed or other factors stand against our petition. The problem is never getting what we want from God as much as getting what God wants from us.

Jesus taught persistence in prayer when he told of man waking up his friend at midnight to ask for bread for an unexpected guest. Naturally, the friend and his family were in bed and their door was locked. With a ring of finality, he said, "Don't bother me ... I can't get up and give you anything" (Luke 11:7, NIV). However, the friend outside kept asking and finally was rewarded. Jesus said, " ... because of his shameless persistence and insistence, he will get up and give him as much as he needs" (Luke 11:8, AMP).

Jesus applied the illustration for his disciples with, "So I say to you: Ask and it will be given to you; seek and you will find; knock and the door will be opened to you. For everyone who asks receives; he who seeks finds; and to him who knocks, the door will be opened" (Luke 11:9–10, NIV).

The three verbs, ask, seek, and knock, appear twice in the two verses. In verse nine, they are present imperatives and, in verse 10, they are present participles. Greek verbs in these tenses can be translated as verbs of continuance. In fact, some Bible versions give that reading.

The Amplified Bible says:

Ask and keep on asking, and it shall be given you; seek and keep on seeking, and you shall find; knock and keep on knocking, and the door shall be opened to you. For every one who asks and keeps on asking receives, and he who seeks and keeps on seeking finds, and to him who knocks and keeps on knocking the door shall be opened (Emphasis added).

Jesus linked the persistence of the man with his friend to prayer and showed the disciples they should ask God repeatedly, if necessary, for the answer to their needs. In Luke 18, He told of a widow who came time after time to a judge to plead for justice. The "unjust" judge in the parable resisted but she kept on coming "for some time" (Luke 18:4). Finally, the judge relented. He said, "Because this widow continues to bother me, I will defend and protect and avenge her; lest she give me intolerable annoyance and wear me out by her continual coming" (Luke 18:5, AMP). The women had no assets or influence to persuade the judge. In fact, women had little standing at all in their culture. Her unfaltering petitions moved him to action.

These accounts do not suggest that God does not want to answer prayer. Jesus Christ is our great High Priest, and He is moved by the "feeling of our infirmities" (Hebrews 4:15). Determination keeps us praying and even growing in faith. We do not beg or cajole Him for relief. The lesson is, if persistence prevails with unjust human benefactors, how much more will our perfect and loving Father come to the aid of His children who never give up?

Jesus closed with, "I tell you, he will see that they get justice, and quickly. However, when the Son of Man comes, will he find faith on the earth?" (Luke 18:8, NIV) The Amplified Version asks here, "When the Son of Man comes will He find (persistence in) the faith on the earth?"

This is important because God's timing may not coincide with our deadlines. His answer may be delayed for reasons only He knows. Luke makes the parable's purpose clear at the start, "Then Jesus told his disciples a parable to show them that they should always pray and not give up" (Luke 18:1, NIV). The Lord knew very well the impatience in human nature. We are geared to quick solutions and easy fixes. Christ honors those who dare to believe Him, no matter how long it takes.

Tested Faith Perseveres

Just as lifting weights builds strength, praying in the face of delays makes us stronger in faith. James said in his New Testament letter, "…you know that the testing of your faith develops perseverance. Perseverance must finish its work so that you may be mature and complete not lacking anything" (James 1:3–4, NIV). He also encouraged believers to ask God for wisdom and promised God would give it generously (verse 5). He even outlines how to present a petition: "But when he asks, he must believe and not doubt, because he who doubts is like a wave of the sea, blown and tossed by the wind" (v. 6 NIV).

If I pray again for what I've already asked of God, is it really a sign of doubt? Not at all! Enduring faith spurs us to keep asking. The widow in the parable kept asking because she believed, or at least hoped, that her request ultimately would be granted. It is not wrong to ask again and again in continuing expectation.

There may be a time when God denies a petition, but I believe that seldom happens without Him giving some insight, encouragement, or instruction. Paul prayed three times for deliverance from what he called his "thorn in the flesh." Then he heard God telling him His grace was sufficient even for a "no" answer to his prayer. Paul said, "Most gladly therefore will I rather glory in my infirmities that the power of Christ may rest upon me" (2 Corinthians 12:9).

Giving God Another Opportunity

When you pray again, you give God yet another opportunity to meet the need. Wesley Steelberg had a terrible heart condition which grew worse, despite prayers by his church and various ministers. He could not continue his duties as a pastor. He attended a campus ministries conference and was asked to say something to the several thousand collegians assembled. As Steelberg came to the stage, the moderator said he felt they all should pray for him. The audience stretched out their hands toward Steelberg, prayed fervently, and witnessed this beloved pastor instantly healed.[8] Steelberg later was elected general superintendent of the Assemblies of God. Recounting this experience many years later at the 1991 Power and Presence Conference, Jack Hayford asked, "What if they had not prayed one more time?"[9]

Would God have healed if they had not prayed? I do not think so. I believe with Hayford that this healing was a gift the Holy Spirit wanted to distribute just then. Yes, He distributes miraculous gifts as He wills, but sometimes we receive them only if we ask.[10]

This healing took place in God's timing, on stage before hundreds of witnesses. Perhaps this was a factor in why healing was delayed. However, as Hayford suggests, without people asking again, the miracle would not have come.

Another example of asking again and receiving came in my own ministry. Cherie and I sang and preached one Sunday in a small church about two weeks after more than ten thousand people had filled an auditorium in a nearby city to hear a well-known evangelist. Great miracles were recorded in the huge meeting, but one brother with a partially paralyzed arm was not healed. It came to him later—that Sunday in his home church. His nearly useless arm was instantly restored.

It obviously was God's will for the man to be healed. He probably had no more faith the night we prayed than at the large meeting. I doubt that I had more faith than, or even as much as, the noted evangelist. What matters is the man gave God another opportunity. He experienced a miracle he may not have received had he not called on God again.

Never hesitate to keep on asking. It is never wrong to keep on believing—to keep on expecting good things from God. If you need healing, do not give up. Keep believing it will happen to you. Every day expect a miracle. I am convinced God delights in our persistence.

THE POWER OF PRAISE
AND WORSHIP

A great way to maintain a patient faith is to cultivate an attitude of worship. Paul taught us to season our petitions with it: "In everything by prayer and petition with thanksgiving present your requests unto God," (Philippians 4:6, NIV). This moves our focus from God's hand to His heart! We do not praise Him because we feel like it but because He is worthy. Praise is not flattery to get what we want. It is true appreciation of the kind of God we serve.

Worship is reverence and homage paid to God. We don't just give it. We owe it, and we do it with both thanksgiving and praise. We thank God for what He has done, and we praise Him for who and what He is.

It is possible to sing about God or mouth words of praise without real worship, but it is impossible to worship without really praising God. Jesus said His Father seeks those who will worship him "in spirit and in truth" (John 4:23). We should make it our goal every day not only to seek Him, but to be the kind of worshippers whom He is seeking. We do that with prayers, songs, and daily lives that reverence and honor Him.

As we continuously acknowledge Christ's presence, our faith grows. Praise and worship help keep the practice of His presence constant. It helps us maintain our focus on God, even when there is no immediate answer to our prayers. The life of worship rises from a deep desire for fresh encounters with God.

Worship and Healing

One of my early personal experiences of healing came when I was a young evangelist preaching revival meetings. A painful growth, perhaps a seed wart, developed on the bottom of my right foot. For nine months, I bandaged my foot every day and cushioned the heel against the stabs of pain which shot through it whenever I stepped down hard.

A doctor could have removed the bothersome mass, but I did not seek medical help. I decided it probably was not life threatening and it was not unbearable. Mostly, I was scared. I cringed at the thought of anyone cutting on my foot.

I realize this problem was not even a blip on the gauge of life's catastrophes, but I also believe God cares about even the little things. Naturally, I prayed about the pain but, eventually, I moved from petition to praise. I determined to praise the Lord for His faithfulness to heal. Each day when I placed the bandage, I would praise Him. I thanked Him because He is my Healer and He had helped me in other situations. It became my everyday routine until one day, after nine months of bandages, the growth was not there! One day it was and the next day it wasn't. Medical experts may explain this as normal with warts but to me, it was an answer to prayer. I also am convinced that sincere praise and worship played a part.

None of this means that praising Him backs God into a corner and obligates Him to help us. Instead, it demonstrates that we grow spiritually when we worship God. Our faith and confidence grow when we concentrate on Christ rather than our problems.

A Bible example appears in Matthew's account of a Canaanite woman who asked Jesus to heal her daughter. She worshiped Him even after an apparent rejection of her petition. The Lord said He had been sent to the "lost sheep of the house of Israel" (Matthew 15:24, KJV). This would leave her out, but she refused to be deterred. "She came and worshiped him, saying, 'Lord help me'" (verse 25). The Lord commended her faith and made her daughter well "from that very hour" (verse 28).

The verses that follow (29–31) may indicate that the woman's faith and Christ's compassion opened a floodgate of healing for many others in the region. They may not have been Jewish, but they glorified the God of Israel. The main point is that we need to learn to worship Him before, during, and after prayer for healing. Most certainly, we should praise Him after we are healed!

Christ also modeled giving praise before making petition when He went to Lazarus's grave. He said, "Father, I thank you that you have heard me" (John 11:41, NIV). Then He commanded Lazarus to come forth.

Praising God—Antidote for Fear

Fear is the enemy of faith. It feeds doubt about the purpose, every promise, and even the power of God. It is natural to be afraid when the doctor brings a negative report or diagnoses a threat to life, but if we give way to fear, it will cripple and torment us. Fear can make it seem impossible to really trust God or even to pray. The antidote is worship!

When we praise the one who knows us best, our Creator, we identify the source of all comfort and help. In worship, we express trust in Him, and we discover that doubts and fears wither in His presence.

King David knew fear, and he knew what to do about it. Captured by an enemy army, he said, "When I am afraid, I will trust in you. In God, whose word I praise, in God I trust; I will not be afraid. What can mortal man do to me?" (Psalm 56:3–4, NIV). Fear cannot be prevented, but it can be conquered. Nothing dissolves doubt like focusing on the Word of God and worshipping the God behind it.

True worship will be constant and consistent. David declared, "I will praise the LORD at all times. I will constantly speak his praises" (Psalms 34:1, NLT). That means he praised God even when he did not feel like it. Sickness and trouble will challenge our choice to worship, but we keep on praising Him. It is vital.

Praise God Anyhow!

"In everything give thanks, for this is the will of God in Christ Jesus concerning you" (1 Thessalonians 5:18, KJV). In every circumstance, God wants us to praise Him. If you are suffering from cancer, praise Him. If trouble persists, praise Him—not because of it but in spite of it! Perhaps no one suffered as much as Job, but he declared, "The Lord gave me everything I had, and the Lord has taken it away. Praise the name of the Lord!" (Job 1:21b, NLT). This great declaration of faith came before there were scriptures for Job to quote and none to read. (Many scholars believe Job was the first of the Bible books to be written.) Job had questions and bitter times of discouragement, especially in the face of miserable comforters, but he never rebelled against God's purpose. It is no wonder God called him "my servant" at the beginning and again at the end of the book, both before and after his suffering (Job 1:8; 42:7–8).

God longs for His people to praise Him. Jesus healed ten lepers but only one returned to thank Him (Luke 17:15–16). Jesus asked, "Didn't I heal ten men? Where are the other nine? Does only this foreigner return to give glory to God?" (Luke 17:17–19 NLT). Obviously, Christ desired all of them to praise Him. This should remind us, especially when blessings are given, to praise the Giver.

The nine who failed to give thanks missed the chance to really know Jesus. They knew Him from a distance. They received the blessing but not the Blesser. They knew healing but not the Healer. True worship brings you into the intimate presence of the Lord. Miracles can occur seemingly just because a person happens to be where Christ's power is manifested. Even unbelievers can be blessed by the general presence of Christ, but the intimate presence of God in worship is the definitive privilege of believers.

Will you praise God like Job, in spite of the fact healing is delayed? Will you continue to praise Him after the healing comes? The race of life is a marathon not a sprint. To build faith and claim victory, we must determine to praise God always!

Hindrances to Healing

Though God expects us to be bold and believing, Satan will try to poison our thinking with questions. He challenges what God can do and whether He even wants to heal. These questions can dwarf our faith and hinder answers to our prayers. Especially when healing is delayed, many fall prey to doubts and false conclusions.

I'm not sure God wants to heal me. The more a person dwells on this thought, the more convinced he or she becomes that God, in fact, does not want to heal. If this were true, God would not have instructed us to ask Him for healing. But He did! James said, "Is any sick among you? Let him call for the elders of the church. And the prayer of faith shall save the sick (James 5:14). Jesus said, "Ask and it shall be given you, seek and ye shall find, knock and it shall be opened unto you" (Luke 11:9, KJV). We understand that God's ways are not our ways and His thoughts are not our thoughts (Isaiah 55:8), but His Word gives us the privilege and the responsibility to believe Him for the impossible.

Maybe God is trying to teach me something by giving me this sickness. The first problem with this rationale is that people who say it do not really believe it. If they did, they would not risk thwarting God's purpose by taking medicine and going to the doctor. They would concentrate on their lesson. If they continue to go to the doctor when they are sick and they continue to use medications for their pain, why should they not keep on praying about their need? Jesus commended doctors (Luke 5:31). They work toward His end, which is healing. It is not wrong to go to the doctor during an illness, just as it is not wrong to keep praying for a miracle.

The second problem with the "God is teaching me" notion is that it is a lie. God does not "give" sickness. Death and disease came into the world because of sin. To argue glibly that God is trying to educate with affliction is to accept a condition He did not create. Satan is the deceiver and destroyer. Sickness is his doing, and Jesus, more than once, recognized a specific sickness as an attack of Satan (Luke 13:16; Acts 10:38). God can bring judgment on His enemies, but His nature is to heal (Exodus 15:26).

Some still would argue, "My sickness is helping me to trust God more." Difficulties should move us to depend more upon God, but a miracle also can boost our faith. We ought not to embrace a position that learns trust only through tragedy. No one would pray, "God, please give me a disease so I can trust you more," or, "Lord, give me cancer so I can be a better servant!" There are far better ways to draw closer to God.

Great testimonies do abound of individuals rising to inspiring heights of faith and accomplishment despite affliction. Fanny Crosby and Joni Eareckson Tada are awesome examples. Millions have been blessed and helped by their triumphant lives in extreme circumstances. God is using their situations to encourage and enable us all to surmount adversity. No doubt, God can use any situation to help bring out the best in us. He empowers us to be faithful and productive despite our physical limitations; however, He does not cause the problems.

What Satan means for evil, God can use for His glory. We should strive to demonstrate tenacity, strength of character, and unwavering faith in the face of suffering, but this does not mean we cannot still thank God for being our Healer. We can and we should continue to give Him opportunity to give us a miracle.

This sickness is just my thorn in the flesh. Some compare themselves to the Apostle Paul and his experience reported in 2 Corinthians. "And lest I should be exalted above measure through the abundance of the revelations, there was given to me a thorn in the flesh, the messenger of Satan to buffet me, lest I should be exalted above measure" (2 Corinthians 12:7, KJV). Paul said he prayed three times for the thorn to be removed, but God spoke to him instead. He gave specific promises of grace to survive and strength to prevail despite Paul's troubles.

Unless you are experiencing abundant revelations and are in jeopardy of being exalted above measure, why would you need a thorn in the flesh? Paul prayed repeatedly for deliverance then deferred to God's will as the Lord told him why he was being afflicted. It is wise to leave this thorny issue with the apostle and best to draw the lessons that God works in us and causes us to prevail despite our limitations.

The passage in question never tells us that Paul's thorn was loss of sight. The numerous efforts to equate Paul's thorn with failing eyesight based on other statements he made concerning the large letters he used (Galatians 6:11) or the Galatians being willing to pluck out their eyes for him (Galatians 4:15) does not justify a supposition of blindness.

Here is Paul's testimony: "And He said to me, 'My grace is sufficient for you, for My strength is made perfect in weakness.' Therefore most gladly I will rather boast in my infirmities, that the power of Christ may rest upon me. "Therefore I take pleasure in infirmities, in reproaches, in needs, in persecutions, in distresses, for Christ's sake. For when I am weak, then I am strong" (2 Corinthians 12:9–10, NKJV).

The apostle learned to trust God in every situation and to be content with or without comforts or even necessities. This does not mean he would have been out of order to call on God for relief. He would stand firm in persecution and rely on Christ's strength to endure no matter what, but nothing implies he would not continue to ask God for provision, protection, and blessing.

We may not understand why we are going through sickness or other troubles, but it is not wrong to ask God to heal and help us. It is good to declare that we are believing God for His intervention. The Israelite captives in Babylon gave us an example. Shadrach, Meshach, and Abednego refused the king's order to worship his golden image. He threatened them with a fiery death, and their response is a classic expression of faith:

If we are thrown into the blazing furnace, the God we serve is able to save us from it, and he will rescue us from your hand, O king. But even if he does not, we want you to know, O king, that we will not serve your gods or worship the image of gold you have set up. (Daniel 3:17–18 NIV)

They said, in essence, "Our God is able to deliver us; we believe He will; but, even if He doesn't, we will trust and serve Him alone." This kind of faith prevails. It does not claim adversity as God's will but commits to trust Him come what may.

I really don't mind my sickness. This may really be the truth. Some people seem to embrace sickness and the attention it may bring. Friends come to visit. Family members cater and sympathizers swarm. Nevertheless, a person should want to be healed. More than our hypochondria gratified, we should want God glorified. We should want the best of health, if for no other reason, that we may better serve the Lord. "For even the Son of Man did not come to be served, but to serve, and to give His life a ransom for many" (Mark 10:45, NKJV).

In the 1960s and 1970s, thousands of people filled huge auditoriums across the nation for healing campaigns where evangelist Kathryn Kuhlman was preaching and praying for the sick. Reports from the meetings drew an invitation for the evangelist to appear on the Tonight Show with host Johnny Carson.

The atmosphere was charged as Carson asked questions about her meetings and the reported miracles. He asked her to agree that most of the sicknesses "healed" were psychosomatic—matters of the mind—and not real physical problems. The audience erupted in applause when Kuhlman breathed her excited response that these are the most difficult kind. With trademark dramatic flair, she suggested it is wonderful that some, at least, get healed of psychosomatic problems. Carson may have been surprised, but he seemed to nod agreement.[11]

Problems may be imagined or they may be real but rooted in the mind or emotions. Whether in the mind or in the body, pain is real and God can heal. Twisted limb or wounded spirit—physical, mental, or emotional woe—every need can be an occasion for God to intervene. We should bring them to Him for relief and for His glory. James tells us to call the elders of the church to pray for us. To fulfill this scripture is to give God an opportunity.

I'm sorry but it's going to take someone with a lot of faith to pray for me. This comment reminds me of the lady who objected when the visiting evangelist started to pray for her healing. "Oh, no you don't! I'm saving that for Oral Roberts!" While the story may have been invented, it is true that some people seem to think only a few special individuals can exercise the kind of faith necessary for them to be healed. In reality, not just the faith of the person praying but the faith of the one prayed for has bearing for the miraculous.

Jesus said to different individuals who had been touched by His power. "Your faith has made you well" (Matthew 9:22, 29; 15:28; Mark 10:52; Luke 7:50; 17:19; 18:42). In fact, He never said, "My faith has healed you" or, even, "My power did the work." Of course, He was the object of their faith and without Him, the miracles would not have come. Still, He encouraged each seeker to have faith so the miracle could happen. Saving faith is in Christ alone. Likewise, faith for healing must be placed in Him and not in any individual He may choose and use.

When Jairus was told his daughter was dead, Jesus said, "Be not afraid, only believe" (Mark 5:36, KJV). Jesus raised her from the dead. Soon afterward, two blind men came and asked Him to have compassion on them. Jesus asked, "Do you believe I can do this?" They said, "Yes, Lord," and the scripture records, "He touched their eyes and said, 'According to your faith let it be to you,' and their eyes were opened" (Matthew 9:29–30a, NKJV). The miracle followed an affirmation of their faith.

In a negative example, the scriptures tell us Jesus could not do mighty works in his own country because of the unbelief of the people (Matthew 13:53–58; Mark 6:5–6). He healed a few sick people but nothing in comparison to what He did elsewhere and what He could have accomplished there if only they had believed. Mark declares that Jesus "marveled because of their unbelief" (Mark 6:6, KJV). Obviously, He expected individuals in need to have faith in Him that great things would happen.

I have discovered that God sometimes honors imperfect faith and even works miracles in spite of the evangelist. I asked a young man in Tolleson, Arizona, why he had come forward for prayer. He said he had blisters on his tongue, and I asked whether he believed God would heal him.

He gave an honest reply, "I just wanted to see if it would work." I must admit, when I heard him, I did not have a lot of faith that anything would happen. I prayed for him and started to pray for the next person in line.

Then, I turned back to ask, "Well, do you believe God healed you?"

He blurted his response. "They're going!" Then, "They're gone!"

He had been able to eat only soup for a week and now he was totally healed! His surprise probably was surpassed only by mine. It clearly was not my faith that touched heaven. God had honored a mustard seed of faith. When the young man gave Him the opportunity, He gave a miracle!

To believe God will respond just to the great faith and powerful prayer of a noted personality is to limit God. We need to recognize that God alone is in charge of how and when He heals. He is sovereign and He also has ordained that individual faith contributes to the process. The candidate for healing, as well as the one praying for that person, needs to believe.

God does call and use individuals for specific ministries, and He confirms His word as they preach and minister in His gifting. However, your faith need not wait until a celebrity arrives. We have an ever-present Healer, and we can call on Him any time. I know people who were healed with the prayer of a child. A missionary friend had been prayed for many times by many ministers and others, but his healing came instantly when his little granddaughter prayed. Not notoriety, but childlike faith, on the part of both the one praying and the candidate for a miracle, most readily moves the hand of God.

What to Do When You Need a Miracle

Faith in God does not mean miracles on demand. God's answers often may not come when or how we want. Here is a biblical and practical "Things to Do" list to help you keep on believing God for a miracle:

1. *Pray when the first pain or indication of sickness appears.* We do not have to wait for the official diagnosis in order to start praying. God knows what is happening, and He is never surprised.

2. *If you get no immediate or complete relief, do not hesitate to seek a doctor's help.* There is no conflict between faith and medicine. Faith is real and God can heal without regard to whether you take medication. Refuse to feel guilty for going to the doctor or taking prescriptions.

When I emphasized this point in a church service, one lady spoke out, "But God told me to flush all my medicine down the toilet and when I did, I was healed."

I replied, "If you *know* God told you to do that, then obey Him, but I will never tell anyone to do it."

It is neither wise nor necessary to stop medications before a doctor confirms healing. Taking medications to relieve symptoms and help you get well in no way contradicts God's purpose or your petition for recovery. Refusing medications is a dangerous practice. It often is really unbelief masquerading as faith and attempting to leverage trust or coerce God. We cannot give Him an ultimatum. One preacher said he told God, "You're going to have to heal me or take me home." To which he said, the Lord replied, "I have your place ready."

We thank God for all the resources and helps available, just as we praise him for a job, but our confidence always is in Him as our source. When healing comes, the doctor will tell you the medications are not needed. Even if he does not recognize a miracle, he can certify the work is done!

3. When the prognosis for recovery is not good or worsens, keep on believing for a miracle. Do not look at the condition but look at the Healer. Stack all your problems against the backdrop of His power. Nothing is impossible with God (Luke 1:37; Mark 10:27).

4. Praise God continually (Psalms 34:1). Sing His praises, shout His praises, think on Him (Philippians 4:8), and speak of His goodness to others.

5. Memorize and pray the scriptures to bolster your faith. Some theologians are reluctant to tell people to do this for fear they may take verses out of context and generate false hope. This is not a problem for the believer who follows Paul's admonition:

"Be diligent to present yourself approved to God, a worker who does not need to be ashamed, rightly dividing the word of truth" (2 Timothy 2:15, NKJV). Reminding God of His word is in line with biblical prayers which often included a recitation of His promises and past provisions (2 Chronicles 20:5–12; Acts 4:25–26). This is not to jog God's memory. Rather, it is to position our needs and petitions in the context of His promises.

6. Stay full of the Spirit. Paul directed believers to "be continuously filled with the Spirit" (Ephesians 5:18, Wycliffe Bible Commentary). Praying in the Spirit keeps our attention focused on Christ. We are instructed to live habitually in the Spirit (Ephesians 5:16, AMP) in order to overcome the limitations of our sin-tainted, carnal nature. "Carnal" means of the flesh—merely physical or material. Our carnal nature wars against our spiritual nature, the God-given capacity to know and relate to Him. We need to stay full of the Holy Spirit so we do not give way to anything that would reason against or impede our faith.[12]

7. Refuse bitterness if the answer is delayed (Ephesians 4:29–31). Doubt and bitterness can overcome you with questions of whether God can, will, or even wants to make you well. Do not let Satan, the father of lies, rob you of your peace or your answer. When the Israelites spoke against God with a mocking challenge, "Can God spread a table in the desert?"

(Psalm 78:19–22, NIV), it obviously did not make Him happy. But He is pleased and His blessings can flow when we nurture a sweet spirit and stand firm in our faith.

WHAT HAPPENS IF NOTHING HAPPENS?

We must pray expecting God to do the impossible. It is the priority in our thinking. We know God will choose His way and His time to answer, but we do not pray with a disclaimer, "What if it doesn't happen?" Instead, we proclaim God is good, loving, and all powerful. We pray always expecting good outcomes.

What should we do though, when the miracle never happens or, as far as we can tell, the answer does not come? Then we keep on trusting God. We believe His promises and we pray in faith, but above all, we trust Him because we know something of His character. He is love itself—merciful and endlessly good and kind. We may not understand what He does or does not do, but we do not question His motives. He works all things together for good to those who love Him and are called according to His purpose (Romans 8:28–29). This refers specifically to the points of redemption Paul was outlining in his letter, but I have found it to be true that He works in everything, good or bad, that comes our way and advances us in His plan. His purpose is to make us like His Son.

God has a perfect track record. In every instance in which we do understand something of His working, He has done for us the best. He deserves our trust in the times we do not understand. When we begin to pray about a need, we place it into God's hands. When our answer does not come, we leave it there.

We do not allow our disappointment to give way to frustration. I have continued to pray for people until they breathed their last breath. The fact they did not receive the miracle I expected does not shake my confidence in God. Neither does it deter me from praying for others. Many, many have been healed but others I prayed for have died. (In fact, all those who were healed will die someday. Lazarus and the others that Jesus raised from the dead died again. Every sick and every well person must know that healing is not the answer to death. The answer to death is the resurrection to eternal life, and that will come to everyone who trusts Jesus Christ as Savior!) I jokingly tell people, "You take your chances when I pray for you because some people I have prayed for died. But take heart, I never had anyone to die on the spot."

I do not try to explain, apologize, or blame someone for lack of faith when what I envisioned does not take place. Instead I maintain my faith in God and encourage people always to keep on believing Him for the impossible.

We will not understand some things until we are in heaven. What we do understand is that we have been commanded to pray believing prayers and we need to keep on doing it. We face the fact that none of us is the Healer, but

He always is in control. We do our best to carry out our tasks and trust Him.

Still No Answer?

The father and family of Seth Trahan are friends I have known for more than twenty years. Seth was a model soldier and a faithful Christian, but he was killed in Iraq. I cannot explain his death. Hundreds of prayers went up for his safety. Yet, he was the only US soldier in Iraq to lose his life on Saturday, February 19, 2005. Does that mean someone failed to pray hard enough? Absolutely not. No one can make sense of such a tragedy. The only solution, and it does not take away the pain, is to leave it in God's hands.

Disappointments will come at times even though we pray, but that does not mean we must quit praying with faith. Answers come from a sovereign God who has told us to ask and expect them. Any exceptions also are in His sovereign hand. We stand as vulnerable prayer warriors. We always pray expecting the impossible. We should never pray perfunctorily, not really believing that anything is going to happen. When we pray fervently and expectantly and it does not seem to turn out right, we open ourselves to questions, doubts, and even greater disappointment unless we trust God implicitly for Who He is.

In his book, *Miracles,* Frank Damazio tells of two women who were diagnosed with cancer. The church dearly loved each of the women, though one was more prominent and public in ministry. He, his wife, and many others prayed intensely for both. One recovered completely but the beloved worker died. Some in the church felt the

Damazios must not have prayed and fasted hard enough. Describing the situation, he wrote:

> *I realized then that the Lord looks at the whole picture, not the effectiveness of a life—and He is God no matter what the outcome of our prayers. We don't pray in order to control God; we pray to partner with His will— even when we don't like it. Does it hurt? Of course. But love must always take the risk of being hurt. As a couple, we've shed many tears over the disappointments of others ... I could protect my feelings and guard my emotions. I could build a hedge around my heart so that I am not affected deeply. To me, this is a coward's approach to the supernatural, not a Christ like approach. Jesus wept when He was standing in front of Lazarus's grave. He felt deeply. He allowed his heart to be touched.[13]*

Cherie and I have seen huge numbers of people healed— more than one thousand in a single campaign! This book reports specifics of many healings we have witnessed and experienced. But no minister who prays for the sick has seen 100 percent made well. Evangelists typically do not report the ones who go away sick. Some explain it away declaring those individuals did not have faith. Ultimately, only God knows why. The important thing is to keep our faith in Him. He will make the call as to when and how to do the work.

The Scriptures link prayer, faith, and positive results. "The prayer of a righteous man is powerful and effective" (James 5:16, NIV). We cannot be effective unless we pray.

We cannot be effective if we draw back from exercising faith. The writer of Hebrews says, "Now the just shall live by faith: but if anyone draws back, my soul has no pleasure in him" (Hebrews 10:38, NKJV). This quotes the Prophet Habakkuk and uses the verse in a sense of shrinking back from the truth for one's eternal well being. It also can be understood that this walk of faith engages every aspect of our lives. We must not pull back from faith for every step of the journey.

THE STEP OF FAITH

I have learned as an evangelist to encourage people to take a step of faith after prayer for their healing. Many times nothing obvious happens when we pray but when they attempt what was impossible before, suddenly they are freed from the disability or disease.

The Lord links His miracle working power intrinsically with active faith. This kind of faith is obedient and willing to take action. It may take the form of trying to do something which, without divine intervention, we cannot do. It may seem foolish or irrational; however, it is interesting and exciting how God responds when we give him an opportunity. Many times He prompts us by His Spirit to attempt what we know is out of the question without His help. Other times, we may not have His nudging, but we give him an opportunity by taking a step of faith in His direction.

This may mean trying to raise a paralyzed arm, trying to breathe deeply if that had been difficult before, trying to walk when we cannot walk, or any number of things we might do after prayer to let God take over.

Clifford's Healing

This happened wonderfully for Clifford, the son of my very close and longtime friends Russell and Ann Skinner. At age twenty-six, Clifford wore a brace on his leg and walked with difficulty and discomfort. The family came to a Sunday night service at North Cental Assembly of God in Houston, Texas, where Pastors Paul and Patricia Emerson joined me in praying for the sick. Clifford came forward and we prayed.

No one instructed him to take off his brace or to take any action other than to believe God. I went on praying for others and the service concluded. The crowd was excited and talking one to another in the church lobby when Clifford said he wanted to take off the brace. He believed God had healed him. He said later that he felt a warm tingling in the leg.

He had not been able to walk without the support, but his parents stood with his faith and allowed him to remove it. He took it off and took a step, then another, and another. God had healed him. Clifford, a special needs individual, still needs prayer for other challenges. But that night he walked away from the brace and now beyond age thirty, he still is walking on a leg that once was crippled.

Bible Examples]

Many individuals in the Bible saw God intervene when they took a step a faith. A classic example, a literal step of faith, is recorded in the third chapter of the Old Testament Book of Joshua. A flooding Jordan River stood between the nation of Israel and their promised land. God gave Joshua their commander the plan of action. He organized the twelve tribes into a procession led by priests carrying the ark of the covenant. This gold-covered chest from the holy place in the tabernacle helped them focus on God's promises, power, and presence. The priests marched toward the swollen river and nothing seemed to happen. They stepped out to step in and *then* God intervened. He stacked the waters on their right, allowed the rest to flow away, and gave them a dry path to their new home. The Bible says:

> *14 So when the people broke camp to cross the Jordan, the priests carrying the ark of the covenant went ahead of them. 15 Now the Jordan is at flood stage all during harvest. Yet as soon as the priests who carried the ark reached the Jordan and their feet touched the water's edge, 16 the water from upstream stopped flowing. It piled up in a heap a great distance away, at a town called Adam in the vicinity of Zarethan, while the water flowing down to the Sea of the Arabah (the Salt Sea) was completely cut off. So the people crossed over opposite Jericho. 17 The priests who carried the ark of the covenant of the Lord stood firm on dry ground in the middle of the Jordan, while all Israel passed by until the whole nation had completed the crossing on dry ground. (Joshua 3:14–17, NIV)*

Ten Lepers Healed

In the New Testament Book of Luke, chapter twelve, Jesus healed ten men with leprosy, but not until they acted on His command. He was entering a village between Samaria and Galilee when the stricken men called out to Him from a distance. They were forbidden to enter the village or to come close to uninfected people. Jesus shouted back for them to go show themselves to the priest. This was the process prescribed by the Law of Moses for a leper to be pronounced clean and restored to society.

No promise is recorded, but the implication is that the priest would declare them clear of the disease. Jesus did not heal them and then say, "Go to the priest." Their expectation had to be based on who He was and what He said rather than any evident change. They risked further humiliation by acting on the instructions of someone who had not examined them at all. They might have been punished for exposing others to the disease. But when Jesus said, "Go," they believed. They acted; they expected something good to happen, and it did.

Something wonderful occured *on the way* to the priest. They took the step of faith and, somewhere along the way, they realized their leprosy was gone.

Medicine and the Step of Faith

Though this point is addressed in chapter fourteen, it needs to be emphasized again. Taking a step of faith does not mean stopping, starting, or changing your medication on your own. Though I encourage people to try to do something they could not physically do before prayer, I never tell anyone to throw away their medicine.

God can heal a person despite the professionally prescribed remedy or medicine he or she may be using. One evangelist prayed for a gentleman who wore thick glasses. He asked God to heal the man's eyesight, but no immediate change was evident. A few days later, the man was driving and his vision suddenly got worse. He could not see clearly so he pulled over on the side of the road. When he removed his glasses, he discovered he now could see perfectly. God healed him in spite of the fact that he still wore glasses. When healing came, it became obvious that the vision prescription no longer was needed.

When an individual feels or believes God has granted healing, he or she should go to the doctor and let the physician make the call. That essentially is what Jesus did in the case of the ten lepers (Luke 17:14). He had them go to the priest to verify that they were healed. This lined up with the Old Testament law (Leviticus 14:1–43). Jesus never contradicted the law of Moses, nor did he ever condemn doctors. Though many physicians in that day prescribed remedies that were ineffective, Jesus did not condemn those who tried to help the sick and dying. Doctors can usually confirm a change in an individual. If for some reason, no change is immediately evident but the person is certain he or she has been healed, continuing to take prescribed medicine is not a sin. Sooner or later, if healing has happened, the change will be evident and your doctor will discontinue medications you no longer need.

SICKNESS AND SIN

Death and all the processes of disease and decay exist because of sin. In a general sense, all sickness comes from Satan since he perpetrated evil on the human race. His ultimate desire is to take away life and land souls in hell. He hates God and everything God cares about, including you and me. Sometimes he attacks directly. In any case, God has given us the answer. Whatever the cause of sickness, Christ is the cure. Satan tries to destroy with worry and fear. He may try to overwhelm us with suffering and trouble. Sometimes we play into his hands and short circuit our own health with wrong choices and harmful habits. In those cases, he likely will be quick to heap on guilt—to suggest, "You don't deserve God's help!" Many individuals begin to believe God is punishing them for some sin, real or imagined.

The good news is that God took care of both sin and sickness on the Cross of Jesus. For spiritual, physical, mental, and emotional healing, Jesus Christ took the punishment to give us peace (Isaiah 53:5). James addressed the sin problem at the same time he instructed prayer for the sick.

[14] Is anyone among you sick? Let him call for the elders of the church, and let them pray over him, anointing

him with oil in the name of the Lord. [15] And the prayer of faith will save the sick, and the Lord will raise him up. And if he has committed sins, he will be forgiven.[16] Confess your trespasses to one another, and pray for one another, that you may be healed. The effective, fervent prayer of a righteous man avails much. (James 5:14–16 NKJV, emphasis added)

Where there is sin, God will forgive. Moreover, He satisfies His own condition for effective fervent praying. By His grace, he makes the person who repents righteous, and it is the effective, fervent prayer of the righteous which avails.

The Apostle Paul explained it this way to the church at Corinth:

17 Therefore, if anyone is in Christ, he is a new creation; old things have passed away; behold, all things have become new. God was in Christ reconciling the world to Himself, not imputing their trespasses to them … 21 For He made Him who knew no sin to be sin for us, that we might become the righteousness of God in Him. (2 Corinthians 5:17–21 NKJV, emphasis added)

Paul, Peter, and James were on the same page when it came to being right with God by faith and overcoming the devil's attacks. Paul wrote:

1 Therefore, having been justified by faith, we have peace with God through our Lord Jesus Christ, 2 through whom also we have access by faith into this grace in which we stand, and rejoice in hope of the glory of God. (Romans 5:1–2 NKJV)

and

1 There is therefore now no condemnation to those who are in Christ Jesus, who do not walk according to the flesh, but according to the Spirit. (Romans 8:1 NKJV)

Peter wrote:

6 Therefore humble yourselves under the mighty hand of God, that He may exalt you in due time, 7 casting all your care upon Him, for He cares for you. 8 Be sober, be vigilant; because your adversary the devil walks about like a roaring lion, seeking whom he may devour. 9 Resist him, steadfast in the faith, knowing that the same sufferings are experienced by your brotherhood in the world. (1 Peter 5:6–10 NKJV)

James urged:

7 Therefore submit to God. Resist the devil and he will flee from you. 8 Draw near to God and He will draw near to you. Cleanse your hands, you sinners; and purify your hearts, you double-minded. (James 4:7–8 NKJV)

Rather than worry about your relationship with God or the source of your sickness, submit to God with repentance and prayer. Resist the devil by citing God's word and claiming His promises. Finally, draw near to God with worship and praise and rest in His hand.

Holding on to Your Healing

It is important to withstand doubt and rebuke Satan while we are praying for a miracle of healing. We also must refute and reject him when he tries to make us doubt after the miracle has happened. If he cannot keep you from receiving from God, he goes to work to reduce the impact. He would like to steal your blessing, and he will do it by telling you nothing really happened.

The pain may return after we have testified of healing. Our first impulse is to assume that nothing did happen, though we obviously were healed. Something like this happened to me soon after I had finished Bible college and was conducting evangelistic meetings.

Preaching nightly services in Augusta, Georgia, I began to experience a pain in my lower back. Though bearable, it was extremely uncomfortable and increasing. Sleeping or sitting was difficult and walking was painful.

I preached each night but spent a lot of time each day asking God to heal me. Realizing my discomfort, Pastor John Moore took me to see his family doctor, and we got in very quickly, even without an appointment (not having to wait was a miracle!). The doctor said I had a growth on the lower part of my spinal column which sometimes happens in men. The growth had burst, giving some relief, but the doctor assured me it would come back with a vengeance. Ultimately, I would need an operation.

"In fact," he said, "I have performed this same operation five different times on one man. After each operation it would always come back." Even more unsettling, he said I would be in bed for a month after surgery.

He was right in that I got better the rest of the time I was in Augusta. My next revival was in Waycross, Georgia, where Gene Cumpton was pastor. One day in his study, I was reading a book by T.L. Osborn. Suddenly the familiar pain hit me in the back. I first recalled the doctor's prognosis and the prospect of surgery. But the book I was reading had built my faith for taking authority over such situations. I shouted out loud, "Devil, you are a liar. In the name of Jesus, I am healed!" And instantly the pain disappeared.

In an evangelistic campaign a few months later in Managua, Nicaragua, with missionaries David and Bonnie Spencer, I gave the testimony of my healing. The central themes of the services were divine healing and salvation. The very next day we took a trip to the other side of the country, traveling some very rough roads until they ended and then continuing by boat to Bluefields, Nicaragua.

Bouncing along in the backseat, I felt sharp pain strike me in the back, the same old pain I had powerfully declared gone just the night before. No one in the car knew the battle I was fighting, but I started to praise God inside. I began to thank the Lord for healing me. As my spirit soared in praise, the pain left me for good. The rest of the trip, I slept in hammocks and bounced around in cars and boats, but the pain was gone. Four decades later, I still am healed! Had I yielded to doubt or fear when the symptoms returned and not rebuked the devil, I am convinced I would not be writing this testimony now.

Satan's Native Language

When Satan attacks, it is time to take the authority God gives us in His word. Like Jesus, we respond to the enemy with, "It is written" (Matthew 4:4, 7, 10), and we cite Scriptures that point to his defeat. We boldly quote what God said to His people—that He is Jehovah Ropheka, "the Lord who heals" (Exodus 15:26). We remind Satan that healing is the "children's bread" (Matthew 15:26) and we are God's children!

Satan is a liar. He invented lying. In fact, Jesus said that lying is the devil's native tongue. "When he lies, he speaks his native language, for he is a liar and the father of lies" (John 8:44, NIV, emphasis added). He will try to convince you that you have not been healed even after a miraculous intervention of the Lord. God's word hammers him with the truth.

Praise and worship, as spelled out in chapter fourteen, is another way to take action against Satan's attacks. Exalting God, we saturate our minds with who and how great He is. When we worship God, our focus turns to His love and faithfulness. We begin to lose sight of ourselves and to bask in His almighty power. Intimate worship restores our peace and trust in Him. It diffuses the self-pity Satan tries to cultivate with his lies.

Satan despises God's people and he is unrelenting in his determination to weaken our resistance, to confuse and afflict us every way he can. He may attack our homes, finances, productivity, and even our health. War with our spiritual enemy is a fact of human life, but our job is just to trust God and leave our situations in His hands. Our sovereign Lord has the final word.

One more thing about hanging on to your healing, use it to serve God. Jesus said to the lame man whom he had healed at the pool of Bethesda, "Stop sinning or something worse may happen to you" (John 5:14–15, NIV). This refers to the continuing and constant process of saying "no" to sinful living. It does not mean perfection but walking in forgiveness and victory, refusing to accept or return to a sinful lifestyle. God did not heal you to become a better sinner. He empowers you to be a better and more effective Christian.

Pass It On!

The Power of Your Testimony

When God does something for you, say so! Telling about it strengthens your Christian walk and impacts others.

Whenever we pray for the sick, I encourage people to report what the Lord has done. Sometimes individuals receive from God but are reluctant to comment. They may be like the woman in Luke 8 who fearfully came forward only after she realized Jesus already knew what had happened. She had reached out to Him in secret faith. She believed she would be healed of chronic hemorrhaging if she just touched the hem of His clothes. She did and she was! When Jesus asked who had touched Him and received a flow of His power, she told him everything in front of everyone.

Jesus's initial reaction was, "Who touched me?"

Peter immediately responded, "Master, the multitudes throng and press You, and You say, 'Who touched me?'" (Luke 8:45, NKJV).

But Jesus was not talking about the jostling of the crowd or an incidental contact. He knew someone had reached out to Him in desperate and determined faith.

Of course, Jesus knew who had touched him, and He could have called her out. Instead, he waited for her to tell her story.

Luke wrote, "Now when the woman saw that she was not hidden, she came trembling; and falling down before Him, she declared to Him in the presence of all the people the reason she had touched Him and how she was healed immediately" (Luke 8:47, NKJV). Then Jesus told her to go her way and that her faith had made her whole.

The only times Jesus told people to keep quiet about their miracle seemed to be when the crowds attracted would actually hinder rather than help during His ministry on earth. He told the man with leprosy in Mark 1:43 not to say anything to anyone, but the man could not keep quiet about his healing. He told everyone around. As a result, *"Jesus could no longer enter a town openly but stayed outside in lonely places.* Yet the people still came to him from everywhere" (Mark. 1:45, NIV, emphasis added). The enthusiastic vocal testimony of the leper hindered Christ's ability to minister in strategic places, such as the synagogues.

In contrast, Jesus told the liberated demoniac of Gadara, "Go home to your family and tell them how much the Lord has done for you, and how he has had mercy on you" (Mark 5:19, NIV). That is exactly what he did.

"So the man went away and began to tell in the Decapolis how much Jesus had done for him. And all the people were amazed" (Mark 5:19–20, NIV). Christ knew He would not return to that Gentile region. Logically, the delivered demoniac could effectively tell his story to the people of Gadara.

John the Revelator recorded an exciting scene in his vision of heaven. He saw saints, holy ones of God, who have overcome Satan the accuser. They prevailed because Christ died for them and they testified of their faith. They were willing to lay down their own lives for Him. Revelation 12:11 says: "And they have defeated him because of the blood of the Lamb and because of their testimony. And they were not afraid to die" (NLT).

Your testimony is most powerful! You are redeemed, bought back to God by Christ's sacrifice, and you have a story to tell of all He does on your journey of faith. Letting other people know solidifies the miracle.

Satan may try to talk a person out of his or her healing, but letting others know helps keep the record straight. Everyone who comes to Christ needs to make a public profession of faith. We also need to make a public profession when He does other mighty works in our lives.

When you tell your story, be concise. Get to the point. Tell what you had, how long it had bothered you, what you could not do before God touched you, and what you can do now (if that is part of your healing). Give God all the glory. If your testimony is lengthy, summarize it and fill in the details later in writing and make it available to others.

When people are healed where I minister, I ask them to write out their testimonies and send them to me. This encourages me and multiplies the witness as I minister to others.

Be accurate and honest in telling what God has done or is doing. Jesus led one man out of town and, in the process of healing, asked whether he could see. The man replied,

"I see men like trees, walking" (Mark 8:24, NKJV). Christ touched him again and then he could see clearly. A partial healing, any improvement, needs to be reported. When individuals say God has touched them but their healing is not complete, we pray again. We give God an opportunity to complete the work.

This has happened for many individuals we have prayed for who were deaf in one or both ears. They begin to hear a little. So, we keep praying and encouraging their faith. The process may take a few minutes but many times, they begin to hear everything. If they receive a partial healing but improve no further at the moment, I urge them to thank God and keep on believing.

I do not pressure people to testify, and I do not tell them they are healed. I may tell them that I will continue to believe with them that the healing has begun. I often confess that I believe God has heard us and that we should expect a miracle. Once, in the middle of a sermon, I stopped and said I felt God wanted to heal someone right then. Marie Cribbs stood at the second pew from the front and I prayed for her. Nothing noticeable happened to her though others were healed. I told her, though, that I wanted her to send me a photo when healing came. Two days later I received this letter:

Hi Bro. Jones,

My wife and I were prayed for at the Sunday morning meeting at Magnolia Assembly in Port Neches when you came and preached. You may remember that we sat just behind you on your right in the congregation.

At any rate, my wife, Marie, who is from Argentina, was prayed for because of Type I diabetes and pain in her shoulder and arm. She hasn't been able to raise her left arm for almost two years due to degeneration from her diabetes while being treated for breast cancer a year and a half ago. After praying for her, you said that you would like a picture of her raising her arms when she was healed.

Last night, we were looking for some things in storage and listening to praise and worship. When we found something that we had been desperately looking for, the music had a crescendo and my wife, without thinking, raised both hands in praise. She realized what had happened and called me into the room. She was able to raise her arm at will for the first time in many, many months! This miracle, I believe, will help her faith for healing of diabetes and psoriatic arthritis.

Thank God for His healing provision! Please find the photo attached, taken moments after the healing! Cribbs

I believe the miracle began that Sunday in church. As of this writing, we are waiting for a report of the rest of her healing, but her faith has been elevated. She continues to believe. In the meantime, she readily shares what God already has done.

No one should testify to healing, or anything else, if it has not happened. There may be times when you have an assurance God has done something, even though nothing has noticeably changed. If so, praise God and keep believing until it physically arrives.

No one should assume or claim God has healed them because someone else said so. In his book, *Authority to Heal*, Ken Blue says,

> *When Christians are prayed over for healing, there is often implicit and sometimes explicit pressure placed on them to report improvement when there is none. This distortion of reality is often the result of some sort of wishful thinking. Or it may spring from a desire to make God or the minister look good.*[14]

God deals with realities and truth. No amount of pressure in a healing service or anywhere should cause us to say there are changes if there are none. On the other hand, we must be willing to report whatever has occurred, not for the benefit of the minister but for the glory of God. If no change has come, we stay steady in our declaration of faith, confident in God, as we await His work of power.

In many overseas campaigns, crowds come because of the miracles. Whether out of curiosity or in hope, they come. Personal testimonies of God's intervention help move others to put their faith in Him. In chapter one, I said Paula Ginn's testimony had influenced twenty-five others to come to Christ in the immediate aftermath of her healing. Many more have been impacted over the years as she has continued to tell of God's mercy and power in interviews, church services, and conversations. This can happen in your life! Your extremity is God's opportunity, and every miracle He performs is an opportunity to introduce others to His goodness.

Questions about Healing

Is Attention on Healing Unwarranted?

Certain Christian denominations feel that any emphasis on divine healing is unwarranted. They represent a group aptly called "cessationists," because they feel that miracles of healing, as well as many other manifestations, ceased with the apostles. This has been addressed to some degree in this book. However, others who may feel that miraculous healings do occur still ask, "Isn't an emphasis on healing unwarranted since our attention should be on the souls of mankind?"

The same Bible that states, "For the Son of Man came to seek out and to save the lost" (Luke 19:10, NRSV), also declares that "…he went around doing good and healing all who were under the power of the devil, because God was with him" (Acts 10:38, NIV).

The first time Jesus sent the disciples out to minister, "he sent them out to preach the kingdom of God and to heal the sick" (Luke 9:2, NIV). He also sent them out with seventy others later (some versions say seventy-two), and He instructed them, "Heal the sick" (Luke 10:9). He trained them to do what He did.

Healing is part of the gospel message. We must not separate what Christ does from who He is. Failing to preach and teach on healing shortchanges those whose faith needs to be nurtured. Omitting any part of the gospel guarantees inadequate results. Those who never hear ministry on witnessing and evangelism, for example, rarely share their faith. Similarly, those who are not taught the healing message seldom experience divine healing. Preaching and teaching on healing allows individuals to give God an opportunity to perform miracles.

What about Generational Curses and Sickness?

One of the first questions doctors will ask someone with heart disease concerns his/her heredity. The same is true concerning many diseases such as diabetes, cancer, cystic fibrosis, and any number of other disorders. Little doubt exists that some maladies persist for generations. The same could be said about sinful habits that seem to be passed on and on, but could I be sick because of some curse on a previous generation? The unequivocal answer stands in what Jesus did by His death on the cross.

Jesus Christ came to destroy the works of the devil, and He did a good job. In the New Testament, the Bible declares that Jesus broke the curse of the law (Galatians 3:13). The power of the cross resolved any hold the past had upon us. The writer of Hebrews said, "We have been made holy through the sacrifice of the body of Jesus Christ *once for all*" (Hebrews 10:10, NIV). Even the greedy and rebellious Old Testament prophet Balaam had to confess that the enemy cannot curse what God has blessed (Numbers 22:12; 23:8, 20).

Some use passages such as Exodus 20:5–6, Deuteronomy 5:8–10, and other Old Testament scriptures to teach that generational curses promised to the third and fourth generations must be broken, even after an individual becomes a Christian. The claim is made that the generational curse must be broken in the Christian's life in order for him/her to be free of sinful habits as well as sicknesses.

The Old Testament passages that deal with generational curses generally are connected with idolatry. But even the Old Testament gave clear instructions of how each individual could be free of any such generational curse (2 Kings 4:6; Ezekiel 18:20–22).

Our sickness is not a result of some punishment God imposes upon us due to the past transgressions of our forefathers. As mentioned earlier, sin can certainly contribute to sickness. But because of Jesus, the Son of God (Hebrews 4:14), the writer of Hebrews exhorted, "Let us then approach the throne of grace with confidence, so that we may receive mercy and find grace to help us in our time of need" (Hebrews 4:16, NIV).

Unforgiveness and Sickness

Sometimes when Christians consistently act carnally, it is easy to declare that they need to be delivered from a generational curse. Paul let it be known that Christians can give place to the devil (Ephesians 4:27). According to 1 Corinthians 3:1, they can be carnal (worldly, NIV) and be guilty of anger, lust, unforgiveness, and any other sin of the flesh. The more they yield to these things, the more Satan attacks them in that area, until they are in bondage. This is not demon possession, which would mean there is no blood covering. Nor does it stem from a generational curse but a willful decision to give place to unrighteousness in one's life. Paul said, "...you are still controlled by your own desires. You are jealous of one another and quarrel with each other. Doesn't that prove you are controlled by your own desires? *You are acting like people who don't belong to the Lord*" (1 Corinthians 3:3, NLT, emphasis added). Such carnality cannot only rob the Christian from the blessings of God, but sickness can result as well. In fact, Paul linked hypocrisy with sickness when Christians took communion and were guilty of sin in their lives (1 Corinthians 11:27–30).

I preached on healing in a church in Oklahoma and then prepared the people for a time of praying for the sick. Prior to inviting the people to come forward, I had the people repeat a prayer after me in order to prepare their hearts to receive from God. In the course of the prayer they were repeating, I heard myself giving them these words, "Lord, forgive me for the bitterness I have in my heart." I didn't know it but there was a lady there for whom that was intended. After I prayed for the sick, I asked for testimonies. One lady came forward and testified that she had not been able to bend over for four years and now she could.

Then she added, "The Lord showed me that I had to get rid of the bitterness and unforgiveness in my heart before I could be healed."

I asked, "How long did you have the bitterness in your heart?"

She replied, "Four years."

Though she had already stated it, I asked her again, "And how long has it been since you bent over?"

She said, "Four years."

Her bitterness and unforgiveness had kept her in bondage physically.

The body is so constructed that constant worry, suspicion, and unforgiving attitudes can cause organs and members of our body to shut down. This does not necessarily mean that God is afflicting us but we punish ourselves through wrong choices. We must be overcomers and be aware of Satan's devices (2 Corinthians 2:11).

Does Satan Have to Ask Permission to Attack Us?

This question stems from the first part of Job in the Old Testament where Satan appeared before the throne of God to ask permission to attack Job (Job 1:6–12; 2:1–7). However, the scriptures do not indicate that God must give his approval each time Satan attacks someone. For example, there is no evidence that Satan asked permission to bind the woman who was bent over for eighteen years. Jesus said matter-of-factly, "And ought not this woman, being a daughter of Abraham, *whom Satan hath bound*, lo, these eighteen years, be loosed from this bond on the Sabbath day?" (Luke 13:16, KJV, emphasis added). Jesus directly attributed the woman's condition to Satan. Satan had attacked the woman eighteen years before Christ came to her rescue.

God has allowed Satan certain parameters since the fall of Adam and Eve (Romans 5:12–14). He is known in scripture as the prince of this world (John 12:31; 14:30; 16:11) and "the ruler of the kingdom of the air" (Ephesians 2:2, NIV). He has the power to "steal and kill and destroy" (John 10:10) but Jesus came to give abundant life (John

10:10) and to "destroy the works of the devil" (I John 3:8).
We are constantly under attack by the prince of this world
but the one in us "is greater than the one who is in the
world" (1 John 4:4). We simply must continue coming to
Jesus, giving Him the opportunity to work on our behalf.

Is Death Itself a Healing?

Some argue that God doesn't heal some because he uses
sickness to take them to heaven. Many Christians do die
of sickness and they are transported into heaven. However,
God is never limited to using sickness to take us into
heaven. It is just as easy for God to call someone home
without sickness as allowing one to go through a painful
illness before his/her death. And it is equally easy for God
to heal the body, regardless of the age of the individual. As
long as we have breath in our bodies, we should continue to
believe God for healing.

Closely related to the above is the idea that when a
Christian who dies with a terminal illness, his/her body is
forever healed. My mother lay in a coma for months prior
to her death. I prayed constantly for her healing. When
she passed away, someone tried to encourage me by stating,
"God answered your prayers. He healed her by taking her
home."

The body we have after this life will be perfect. There
will be no more pain or sickness (Revelation 21:4). However,
the resurrected body will be different from this earthly body,
just as Jesus's body was different after His resurrection. He
appeared and disappeared at will (Luke 24:31; John 20:19).
Our bodies will be like His (1 John 3:2). In my opinion, it is
not a physical healing that one receives when passing on to

heaven. The Spirit goes to be with Him. The body awaits its transformation after the return of Christ to catch us away. (See 1 Thessalonians 4:15–18, particularly verse fifteen, which suggests that the spirit of man will come back with Christ to be reunited with the body.) The Christian will then experience a spiritual transformation which will result in a new body.

Death, for believers in Christ, ultimately will be transcended with glorious bodies we will have in heaven. However, that transformation differs from a healing of our natural bodies. It is correct and comforting to say, "They never received their healing here on earth, but now they are free from suffering forever."

Regardless of how we express it, our ultimate goal on earth is to please God in these earthly bodies. He is delighted when we believe Him and pray for miracles. When we arrive in heaven, I am sure we will wish we had been there sooner. Either way we can't lose.

Appendix:
countdown to a miracle

Monday	Let someone know about your need who will agree with you in prayer	Pray at least 30 minutes. Mix with prayer and worship.	Read Mt. 8	Memorize Mt. 8:16	FAST AT LEAST ONE MEAL ON ONE OF THESE DAYS
Tuesday	Have 30 minutes of prayer and praise.	Stay in an attitude of prayer all day.	Read Mt. 9	Memorize James 5:14, 15	
Wednesday	30 minutes of prayer and praise.	Maintain an attitude of prayer all day.	Read Mark 7:24-37	Memorize Psalms 103:3	
Thursday	30 minutes of prayer and praise	Stay focused on God throughout the day.	Read Luke 7:1-22	Memorize Mark 11:24	
Friday	Prayer and Fasting	Continuous praise and worship	Read John 11:1-45	Memorize 1 John 5:14-16	Pray for someone who is sick who will be prayed for on Sunday.
Saturday	Try to pray at least an hour	Continuous praise and worship	Read Acts 3:1-11; 14:8-10	Memorize John 15:7	Go over all memorized scriptures.
Sunday	Get up early to pray. Be worshipful prior to service.	Allow your faith to grow.	Keep repeating memorized Scripture.	Expect the impossible to happen.	RECEIVE YOUR MIRACLE!

PRAY IN THE SPIRIT EACH DAY

NOTES

1 Luke 13:10–17.

2 Charles H. Kraft, "A Third Wave Perspective on Pentecostal Missions," Called and Empowered, eds. Murray A. Dempster, Byron D. Klaus, and Douglas Petersen (Peabody, MA: Hendrickson, 1991), p. 304.

3 Francis MacNutt, Healing (Notre Dame: Ave Maria, 1974), p. 53.

4 Oral Roberts, William DeArteaga, Paul Thigpen, and Jack Deere, Miracles Never Cease (Lake Mary, FL: Creation House, 1991), pp. 55–56.

5 Some modern translations omit or footnote Mark 16:9–20 as missing from two of the oldest manuscripts. They appear in some respected early codices as well as most of the later manuscripts. They also are quoted by the early fathers as far back as the second century. (See John Rea, Bible Handbook on the Holy Spirit [Orlando, FL: Creation House, 1998], pp. 116–117). These verses were included in the manuscripts of the early church councils when they confirmed the Sacred canon.

6 On two occasions Michael, the archangel, said, "The Lord rebuke you" when addressing Satan. Perhaps we

should say it the same way instead of "I rebuke you, Satan." At any rate, the rebuke was vocalized.

7   Everett F. Harrison, "Romans," The Expositor's Bible Commentary, ed. Frank E. Gaeblein, (Grand Rapids: Zondervan Publishing House, 1976), p. 114.

8   "The Power and the Presence," Leadership (Summer, 1991): 14.

9   Ibid.

10 Ibid.

11 Interview, Tonight Show with Johnny Carson, October 15, 1974.

12 Doyle Jones, Be Filled With The Spirit (Mustang, OK: Tate Publishing, 2006), pp. 63-70.

13 Frank Damazio, Miracles (Portland, Oregon: City Bible Publishers, 2004), p. 84.

14 Ken Blue, Authority to Heal (Downer's Grove, IL: Intervarsity Press, 1987), p. 131.

Selected Bibliography and Related Materials

Aker, Ben. "Initial Evidence, A biblical Perspective," pp. 455-459. *Dictionary of Pentecostal and Charismatic Movements*. Eds. Stanley M. Burgess and Gary B. McGee. Grand Rapids: Zondervan Publishing House, 1988.

Chappell, Paul. "Great Things He Hath Done: Origins of the Divine Healing Movement in America" Ph.D., diss. n.d.

Cook, W. Robert. *The Theology of John*. Chicago: Moody Press, 1979.

Duling, Dennis C. and Norman Perrin, *The New Testament: Proclamation and Parenesis, Myth and History*. 3rd. edition. Ft. Worth, TX: Harcourt Brace College Publishers, 1994.

Ervin, Howard M. *Spirit Baptism*. Peabody, MA: Hendrickson Publishers, 1987.

Garlock, H. B. *Before We Kill and Eat You*. Dallas, TX: Christ for the Nations, 1974.

Gee, Donald. *The Fruit of the Spirit.* Springfield, Missouri: Gospel Publishing House, 1928.

Harris, Ralph W. *Spoken By the Spirit*. Springfield, MO: Gospel Publishing House, 1973.

Holdcroft, L. Thomas. *The Holy Spirit, A Pentecostal Interpretation*. Revised Edition. Abbotsford, Canada: CeeTeC Publishing, 1999.

Horton, Stanley M. *The Book of Acts*. Springfield, MO: Gospel Publishing House, 1994.

Horton, Stanley M. *What the Bible Says About the Holy Spirit*. Springfield, MO: Gospel Publishing House, 1976.

Palma, Anthony D. *The Holy Spirit, A Pentecostal Perspective*. Springfield, MO: Gospel Publishing House, 2001.

Rea, John. *Bible Handbook on the Holy Spirit*. Orlando, FL: 1998.

Reed, D. A. "Oneness Pentecostalism," pp. 650–651. in *Dictionary of Pentecostal and Charismatic Movements*, Eds. Stanley M. Burgess and Gary B. McGee. Grand Rapids: Zondervan Publishing House, 1988.

Sherril, John. *They Speak With Other Tongues*. Grand Rapids: Baker Book House, 1964.

Stronstad, Roger. *The Charismatic Theology of Luke*. Peabody, MA: Hendrickson, 1984.

Synan, Vinson. Personal Interview (February 4, 2005).

Synan, Vinson. *The Century of the Holy Spirit*. Nashville: Thomas Nelson Publishers, 2001.

Wagner, Peter. Cited in H. V. Synan. *The Spirit Said Grow*. Monrovia, CA: MARC, 1992.

Warner, Wayne, Ed. *Touched By The Fire*. Plainfield, NJ: Logos International, 1978.

ABOUT THE AUTHOR

Doyle Jones has served as pastor, educator, and missionary, but he is best known as an evangelist whose ministry has taken him to most of Latin America and to many other areas of the world. Influenced by the late Missionary/Evangelist Richard Jeffrey and others, he dedicated his missionary efforts to establishing churches through an evangelistic ministry which emphasized the miraculous.

Dr. Jones received his Bachelor of Arts from Southwestern Assemblies of God University (SAGU), Waxahachie, Texas. He later earned a Master of Divinity from Assemblies of God Theological Seminary, Springfield, Missouri and completed his Doctor of Ministry at Oral Roberts University, Tulsa, Oklahoma. In 1991, Dr. Jones returned to SAGU to assume the position of Director of Missions for his alma mater, a position he held for fourteen years.

Doyle and his wife, Cherie, a pastor's daughter, have dedicated their lives to evangelistic ministry. Together they have planted over forty churches in other countries and have seen multitudes come to Christ. One church he started in Nicaragua now runs over 25,000. Dr. Jones has traveled extensively in America preaching powerful evangelistic messages throughout the United States. He has seen thousands of individuals miraculously healed at home and abroad.

Jones is well suited to writing a book of this nature. His theological training as well as the numerous miracles he has witnessed combine for a balanced teaching on the subject of healing.

Jones is married to Cherie, the daughter of former Assemblies of God pastors, Reverend and Mrs. Lonnie Fogger (both deceased). The Jones's have two sons, Donovan and Nathan, who are pursuing careers in the ministry.

OTHER WORKS
BY DR. DOYLE JONES

Be Filled with the Spirit
from Tate Publishing

Available at www.tatepublishing.com/bookstore

Forever Relevant: Yesterday, Today, and Tomorrow

From Faith Printing Company

Available at www.doylejonesministry.com

For more information or to order books
and/or CDs from Doyle Jones please contact:

Doyle Jones
PO Box 182
Waxahachie, TX 75168

www.doylejonesministries.org
cherieljones@sbcglobal.net